The apparitions of
Garabandal

To my mother (d. Feb. 8, 1961)
from whom I first learned to love
the Blessed Virgin.

THE AUTHOR

I

*The original book was published
in Spain under the title*

**LAS APARICIONES
NO SON UN MITO**
el interrogante de Garabandal

LIBRARY OF CONGRESS CATALOG NO. A 879-508

Publishing history

Spain:	August 1965 & 3 later editions	
France:	December 1965 & 2 later editions	
Mexico:	1966	
Germany:	1966	
Argentina:	1966	
Italy:	1967	
U.S.A.	November 1966	first edition
	August 1967	second edition
	September 1969	third edition
	May 1970	fourth edition
	March 1971	fifth edition
	May 1972	sixth edition
	August 1973	seventh edition
	June 1975	eighth edition
	May 1976	ninth edition
	May 1978	tenth edition
	March 1979	eleventh edition
	November 1981	twelfth edition
	May 1984	thirteenth edition
	July 1989	fourteenth edition
	October 1991	fifteenth edition
	April 1994	sixteenth edition
	March 1997	seventeenth edition
	October 2000	eighteenth edition
	May 2019	nineteenth edition

Copyright © 1966 by
ST. MICHAEL'S GARABANDAL CENTER
FOR OUR LADY OF CARMEL, INC.
889 PALO VERDE AVE.
PASADENA, CA 91104 U.S.A.

www.garabandal.org

LITHO IN U.S.A

F. SANCHEZ-VENTURA Y PASCUAL

The apparitions of
Garabandal

Translated from the Spanish
By
A.   De Bertodano

ST. MICHAEL'S GARABANDAL CENTER
FOR OUR LADY OF CARMEL, INC.
889 PALO VERDE AVE.
PASADENA, CA 91104 U.S.A.

www.garabandal.org

The name of Garabandal, the village of the Apparitions, is becoming well known throughout the world. San Sebastian de Garabandal, to give it its full name, is a small village lost in the Northeastern mountains of Spain, where seventy families lead a hardy existence, some 90 kilometers (55 miles) from Santander. None but detailed maps show its location, and it is easy for the unwary traveler to mistake for *San Sebastian de Garabandal*, the resort town of *San Sebastian*, which lies a little further along the Atlantic coast, near the French border.

Ever more frequently, notices were seen to appear in the Press, relating strange events, prodigies, conversions, as well as messages attributed to Saint Michael the Archangel and the Blessed Virgin Mary. Controversy sprang up around these events, especially in Spain and France, where it became difficult for the layman to sift out the facts, unless he was able to travel to Garabandal and find out for himself.

At last, Mr. Monroy, the Editor of a Tangier newspaper, *La Verdad,* sparked a reaction by making public his utter disbelief in *all* apparitions which, according to him, were nothing but a pure myth. An interested lawyer, who also holds the Chair of Economics and Legislation at the University of Saragossa, refuted these arguments in a book which, in Spain, was published under the title of "Apparitions are not a myth — The enquiry into Garabandal."

This is the book which we are now presenting, thus making available to the English-speaking public on this Continent all the carefully gathered documentation of an author whose professional experience was likely to make, more than anyone else perhaps, a sober, cautious and trustworthy witness.

For ease of reference, the author broke down the material of this book into small sections numbered from 1 to 70 — this edition preserves the author's section numbering system. The original book however, opened with a rebuttal of Mr. Monroy's arguments which are not of such burning interest here as they are in Spain. It was thought preferable to transfer the first two chapters of the Spanish edition (sections 3 thru 11) to the end of this book, where they will be found under Appendix A and B.

AUTHOR'S NOTE

The author solemnly declares that this book has been submitted to eminent theologians and official censors, and that all the corrections they suggested have been included.

In spite of this however, and in response to valid suggestions to that effect, it was decided at the last minute not to apply for the "imprimatur", to avoid placing the ecclesiastical authority before a request for approval of a book that contains the relation of certain events that have not yet received official sanction. Such an "imprimatur" might have been interpreted by some as an implicit acknowledgement by the Church of the supernatural origin of a series of phenomena that are still under examination.

In due obedience and submission to the hierarchy, the author places this book unconditionally in the hands of the ecclesiastical authority, and hereby declares that he is prepared to omit or modify whatever that authority may wish to see omitted or modified; he accepts the ecclesiastical authority's decisions for or against Garabandal, as and when the matter is brought to a conclusion. He also offers to withdraw this publication at the slightest suggestion to that effect on the part of the Archbishop of the diocese to which he belongs.

F. S-V. y P.

ACKNOWLEDGEMENTS

I should like to acknowledge the invaluable assistance given me in compiling this book by many eyewitnesses of the events recounted in these pages.

Through them, I was able to gather countless reports, films, letters, photographs, tape recordings and other testimony of all kinds, the very abundance of which served to cross-check their authenticity and enabled me to write the short account which I now present in newspaper report style.

My heartfelt thanks to them all, and very particularly to the Marqués and Marquesa de Santa Maria, Dr. Gasca and Dr. Ortiz, Don Placido Ruiloba, Don Alejandro Damians, Don Jose Maria Concejo, Don Maxima Foerschler, Señorita Carmen Cavestany and Señorita Ascencion de Luis.

At the same time as expressing my gratitude, I should like to offer to them, without prejudice to my author's rights, any possible profits the sale of this book may bring, to be made available for whatever work they may consider most suitable among the many that are now, or will later be devoted to spreading and publicizing the messages of the Blessed Virgin.

My sole intention in so doing is to follow the example that I have always been given by this splendid group of friends and helpers of selfless zeal and enthusiasm for their magnificent apostolic work.

F. S-V. y P

CONTENTS

R.P. Gustavo Morelos
P R E S E N T E.

Estimado Padre:

Teniendo en cuenta las indicaciones de la Santa Sede y del —
Excmo. Ordinario de Santander (España), así como lo prescrito por el Código
de Derecho Canónico, aprobamos y bendecimos la publicación del Mensaje de —
la Sma. Virgen en San Sebastián Garabandal en nuestra Arquidiócesis, sabien
do de que, a la luz de la Divina Revelación, nos urge la necesidad de la ora-
ción y del sacrificio, del culto a la Sagrada Eucaristía y a la Sma. Virgen
María, y la obediencia, amor y adhesión filiales al Vicario de Cristo y a —
la Sta. Iglesia.

Por consiguiente, no encontramos en este Mensaje, atribuido a
la Sma. Virgen, nada contrario a la Fé y a las costumbres, y sí oportunas,
útiles y saludables amonestaciones para obtener la salvación eterna.

La obediencia en acatar pronta y filialmente las disposicio-
nes de la Iglesia, ha sido la característica de las personas que han sido —
favorecidas en estas apariciones, y por tanto, es una clave segura para to-
dos, de que Dios está aquí.

La prudencia de la Sta. Iglesia en relación a este importante
asunto, se ha manifestado en el estudio atento y pastoral vigilancia, y de
ninguna manera, en prohibición y rechazo del mismo.

Uno de los Oficiales de la Sagrada Congregación de la Defensa
de la Fé, Mons. Philippi, declaró al Revmo. P. Elías, Superior del Carmelo
en la Ciudad de Puebla, que lo consultó en Roma sobre las apariciones de la
Sma. Virgen en Garabandal, que el hecho de que el P. Pío, reconocido por su
virtud, ciencia y adhesión a la Santa Sede, apruebe estas apariciones, y —
aliente a las 4 niñas Videntes a propagar el Mensaje de la Sma. Virgen, es
una grande prueba de la veracidad de las mismas.

Dado en Jalapa de la Inmaculada, 8 de Julio de 1966

+ Manuel Pío López

Manuel Pío López, Arzobispo de Jalapa

VIII

To:
Rev. Gustavo Morelos,
C I T Y

Dear Father:

Keeping in mind the indications of the Holy See and of His Excellency the Bishop of Santander, as required by Canon Law, we give our approval and blessing to the publication in our Archdiocese of the Message of the Most Blessed Virgin Mary at San Sebastian de Garabandal, knowing as we do, in the light of Divine Revelation, that we are urgently required to practice prayer, sacrifice and devotion to the Holy Eucharist and the Most Blessed Virgin Mary, and to display filial obedience, love and faithfulness towards the Vicar of Christ and the Holy Church.

We consequently find nothing in this Message, attributed to the Most Blessed Virgin Mary, that is contrary to the Faith or morals; rather do we note its opportune, useful and beneficial admonitions for the attainment of eternal salvation.

Prompt and filial obedience to the provisions of the Church has been the characteristic of the privileged persons in these apparitions, and this is a sure mark of God's presence for everyone to see.

The Holy Church showed its wisdom in relation to these important events by giving them careful study and by exercising pastoral vigilance; it did not issue any kind of prohibition or rejection.

One of the Officials of the Sacred Congregation for the Defense of the Faith, Msgr. Philippi, who was consulted in Rome by the Very Rev. P. Elias, Superior of the Carmel of the City of Puebla, on the subject of the apparitions of the Most Blessed Virgin at Garabandal, stated that the fact that Padre Pio -- well known for his virtue, his knowledge and his faithfulness to the Holy See --acknowledged these apparitions, and encouraged the 4 Visionaries to spread the Message of the Most Blessed Virgin, was great proof of the authenticity of these apparitions.

Given at Jalapa de la Inmaculada on the 8th of July 1966
Manuel Pio López, Archbishop of Jalapa (Mexico)

Introduction

1.— Señor Juan Antonio Monroy recently published a book called "El Mito de las Apariciones," or "The Myth of Apparitions." On the cover was a photograph of the persons involved in the supposedly miraculous events at Garabandal. The book was published in Tangier by Editorial Pisga. And on the very first page there stands out starkly a definition by Ethelbert Stauffer which is taken as a motif: "What is myth? . . . Myth", he replies, "is the language of all religion."

Monroy, editor of the newspaper "La Verdad", has taken the seemingly miraculous happenings at San Sebastian de Garabandal as a pretext to write what is nothing less than a blatantly violent attack on the apparitions of the Blessed Virgin Mary. To Monroy's mind, San Sebastian de Garabandal is no different from Lourdes and Fatima, which he considers a quagmire of contradictions and skillfully baited pitfalls laid by the Church to trap the unwary.

His book is written in the easy narrative style of the man in the street, and it is precisely as a man in the street that I feel obliged to counter it. I am interested in the subject of apparitions, too. In 1961, I wrote a book entitled "Estigmatizados y Apariciones" (Stigmata and Apparitions), in which I delved into these incomprehensible occurrences in the world of the supernatural.[†] Monroy and I are not theologians, and we probably both lack sufficient grounding to be able to deal authoritatively with matters of this nature. The subject intrigues us both, however, and we have likewise both studied it and then taken the daring step of publishing the fruits of our investigations. But there is one fundamental difference between us. Monroy (so he says) believes in God alone, and in the Bible. The author of this book, for his part, feels fortunate in believing in everything else, too. As a practicing Catholic, I accept all the Church's decisions with sincere and humble faith. Consequently, even before studying the subject, I firmly believed in the apostolate of the Blessed Virgin through her apparitions, and since I began examining them, my faith has strengthened and

---

[†] Further proof of the interest that the author has always taken in visions is the fact that, on August 31st, 1964, the *Teatro Pereda* in Santander saw the premiere of his play called *"Mensaje de Luz, El Misterio de Fatima"*, performed by the Mary Carrillo Company. The author used the nom-de-plume of Ventura del Val.

my enthusiasm grown. I firmly believe in Our Lady of Paris and in La Salette, in Lourdes and in Fatima, etc. And, after what I have seen and experienced there, I also believe that, at San Sebastian de Garabandal, there have taken place, and still are taking place, a series of phenomena beyond any natural explanation . . .

Since Monroy has taken Garabandal as a pretext for an attack on the Catholic Church, I shall similarly take the defense of the Church as sufficient reason to print a simple, bystander's account of the events that have occurred, and still are occurring, at this little Cantabrian village. For the happenings at Garabandal have not fizzled out like a damp squib, as some would like to make out. Far from it. Garabandal is, to my mind, very much alive. The story grows ever more exciting with the promise of a public miracle to be announced in advance when the time comes. Indeed, if the events related here are not due to supernatural causes, then this very promise will be the undoing of Garabandal. Unless their prophesies were unquestionably true, what need had these little girls to make such a prediction, which would only serve in the long run to give away the whole farce?

2.—In the opening chapters of this book,[†] I intend to reply to Monroy's attacks on the Church and on those apparitions that have been officially approved by the ecclesiastical authorities. In the second part, I shall give the reader a brief account of the incidents at Garabandal (although in all cases with the reservations necessary when speaking of inexplicable events not yet sanctioned by the Church).

The second part will be submitted to the Church censors, as was my previous book *"Estigmatizados y Apariciones"*, which received their approbation. This does not imply, however, that the censors' approval of my book is tantamount to recognition of the supernatural causes of these phenomena, which must still continue to be investigated at great length. Hence, when I use such terms as "vision," "ecstasy", "rapture", "Blessed Virgin", etc., they are to be understood simply in respect of what the eyewitnesses say and hear, and the reader should not take them to be an assertion of a proven fact.

But, in the light of Monroy's ruthless attacks, conscience moves me to counter his affirmations with a simple chronicle as objective, sincere and fair as possible, keeping in mind that, under certain circumstances, an omission can be as misleading as outright deception . . .

---

† Now transferred to Appendix A and B

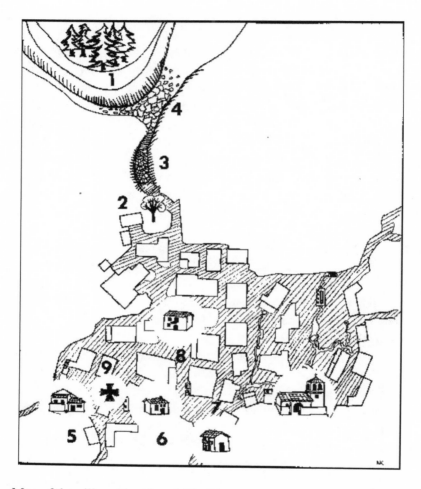

Map of the village showing 1 The Pines 2 The apple tree 3 the "cuadro", where the Archangel St. Michael first appeared 4 The "calleja", or sunken lane 5 Conchita's house 6 Jacinta's house 7 Maria-Cruz' house 8 Loli's house 9 The scene of the Miracle of the Host

Chapter One

REASONED ARGUMENTS TO FAN THE FLAMES OF OUR FAITH

12—In the apparitions known as those of Our Lady of Paris, the Virgin forewarned Sister Catherine Labouré of the disasters that would befall France and the world at large. "The time is near when there will be great danger," Our Lady said. "Everyone will believe all to be lost. I shall be with you all. Have trust in Us. Do not fear."

In these terms Our Lady of Paris made an appeal from heaven for faith and hope. The Virgin asked people to have recourse to her ... On her fingers she wore rings covered in precious gems which gave off flashing rays of light. "The rays of light," she explained, "are the graces which I give those who ask me for them." Then, an oval frame formed around the vision, and on the border there appeared the following words in golden letters. "Oh Mary conceived without sin, pray for us who have recourse to thee."

"Then," Sister Laboure recounts, "I heard a voice saying to me, "have a medal struck according to this picture. All those who wear it will receive great graces; these graces will be abundant for those who wear it with faith . . .[†]

On this occasion, the Blessed Virgin was presented as the mediator of

---

[†] The front of the medal bears an image of Our Lady with her hands stretched out and downwards, and from them proceed rays of light, symbols of the graces granted by her. She is standing on the globe of the world, around which is coiled the serpent which squirms as it is crushed. Around the frame can be seen the words, "Oh Mary conceived without sin, pray for us who have recourse to thee". So, the Blessed Virgin appears as Mother Immaculate, victorious over evil and Queen of the Universe. On the back of the medal is further consolation in symbolic form. Mary's initial "M", surmounted by a cross standing on a cross bar. Below are two hearts, one crowned with thorns and the other pierced by a sword. The Hearts of Jesus and Mary united in their common mission of expiation for mankind. The Kingdom of the Son of God is thus based on the kingdom of Our Blessed Mother, which serves as a triumphal chariot. These are the symbols and meaning of the miraculous medal which awoke religious fervor in France and spread it throughout the world. This was the first apparition of the 19th century, and from this moment there began an movement of mankind towards God.

heaven. She announced disasters, but she assuaged the fears of her children, promising them her assistance, and offered to grant the graces that they requested with faith. Our Lady's words were to be fulfilled to the letter. This was the pointer for all.

Once the medal was struck, its use spread like wildfire. All those wearing it with faith obtained the graces that they requested. Despite the general coldness towards religion, and the skepticism spread by the French Revolution, the reaction of the faithful was astonishing. For us, as human beings, this is the best proof of its authenticity. The Abbé Guillion published the story of the medal in a book called "Nouvelle Historique", of which five editions had to be printed in a single year to meet demand. The medal was at first turned out at a rate of more than a hundred thousand a month, but this proved insufficient, and production soon soared into the millions.

In one of Sister Catherine's descriptions of the vision, she comments on the sentence, "Mary is Queen of the Universe and of each one of us individually." She adds: "It will be a long-lasting period of peace, joy and happiness. *She will be carried in triumph and will travel around the world."*

Here, to my mind, is a prophesy that has already come true. The title of the book in which it appears is *"La Vénérable Catherine Labouré"*, published in France by Edmund Crapez. That *triumphal tour of the globe by Mary* seems a clear allusion to the journey of Our Lady of Fatima, whose pilgrim statue travels incessantly to all parts of the world.

In the apparitions of Our Lady of Paris, there is one circumstance that has been repeated at Garabandal.[†] As Our Lady left Sister Catherine after her final vision, she said to her: "You will not see me again, but you will hear my voice in your prayers." When the visionaries at Garabandal ceased to have visions, they began to experience this new mystical phenomenon, supernatural locutions in which they held an inward conversation with Our Lady, "hearing her voice without words."

But the story of the Miraculous Medal would not be complete without the case of the conversion of a young Jewish banker, Alphonse Rathisbonne. After making a name for himself through his hatred of Catholics following his brother's conversion—and subsequent ordination in the Society of Jesus— providence dictated that Alphonse should go to Rome, where he met an acquaintance, the Baron de Bussières. De Bussieres told him numerous amazing
stories of occurrences connected with the Miraculous Medal, and begged him to accept one, eliciting from him the promise to wear it. Rathisbonne made it

---

[†] See Section 20 in connection with Locutions

clear that it was a waste of time, since he was a Jew and would die a Jew. But they came to a strange agreement. As proof of the fact that he had not faith in the medal and was not afraid of its "marvelous powers," Rathisbonne promised to wear it round his neck and even to invoke it from time to time.

That promise was the cause of the prodigy, for Rathisbonne himself had a vision of the Blessed Virgin and was converted to Catholicism under most extraordinary circumstances. After so many years of open hatred of priests in general, and Jesuits in particular, he finally followed in his brother's footsteps and entered the Society of Jesus.

The extraordinary circumstances surrounding this much publicized conversion, of which ample records exist, are yet further pointers helping men on the way to belief.

La Salette (1846)

13—A brief glance at Our Lady of La Salette, simply covering a number of the most convincing arguments, the cases or circumstances that best serve to uplift our faith. Ordinary mortals are like St. Thomas and need to be able to touch Christ's wounds with their hands to believe. God understands this need of our reasoning minds and constantly provides us with tangible proof of the existence of the supernatural.

At La Salette, Melanie Calvet, aged fifteen, and Maximin Guiraud, aged twelve, suddenly saw a globe of motionless light. This opened out, and inside they saw another, brighter moving light. Within this radiant orb was Our Lady.

"If my people will not submit," she said to them, "I shall be forced to let the arm of my Son fall on them." *And she listed a whole series of calamities that were threatening the world.*

"If sinners repent, the stones and rocks will turn into heaps of wheat, and potatoes will be sown by themselves." Here again, the message confirmed the connection existing between sin and suffering, the state of grace and peace; the whole concept being applicable, not only to the other world, but to this one, too. "The stones and rocks will be turned into wheat. . . "

This doctrine is not a new one. In Exodus (XV, 26) we read "If thou wilt listen to the voice of the Lord thy God, and obey his commandments, and observe all that He bids thee observe, then I will never again bring upon thee all that misery I brought upon thee in Egypt."

Were those perils, foretold in 1846, subsequently confirmed by historical events, or not?

The Blessed Virgin announced that *by Christmastide there would be no potatoes left* because of the total failure of the crop. So it came about that

15

peasants all over France and abroad, particularly in Ireland, began to suffer from acute starvation as winter progressed. The French newspaper *"Gazette du Midi"* of January 28th, 1847, and the London papers of January 21st, of the same year told the sorry tale. "The losses caused by the failure of the crops in Ireland alone are estimated at twelve million pounds sterling, the equivalent of three hundred million francs."

"The wheat will be worm-eaten and will fall into dust," said Our Lady. And, true enough, in 1851, disease attacked the grain crops and caused incalculable losses throughout Europe. *L'Univers* wrote, on July 15th, 1856, "We opened a few dry ears of wheat. Some did not contain a single grain; others held very small grains, totally unfit to feed anyone. In both types of ears, we found a yellowish dust and a few little insects which are undoubtedly the cause of all these ravages. Anyone can see this new phenomenon for himself in any wheat-field ...

"There will be a great famine . . . Some will do penance through hunger." The price of wheat in 1854 and 1855 rose to sixty francs a hundredweight, and, according to *"Le Constitutionnel"* and *"L'Univers,"* in 1856, a hundred and fifty-two thousand people died of starvation in France alone, while other papers gave an estimate of more than a million in all Europe. On December 12th, 1856. *"L'Univers"* said: "For the euphemism 'death caused by want,' read: 'died of misery and hunger'."

The Spanish Government bought sixty million reals-worth of wheat to stave off starvation. In Poland, the Government raised its civil-servants' salaries by a third to help them meet soaring food prices.

"Little children will be seized with trembling and will die in the arms of those who are holding them ..." The prophesy began to come true in 1847, in the canton of Corps. In 1854, all over France seventy-five thousand died of ague. The symptoms were an icy coldness which later made the child perspire copiously, causing a constant shivering and bringing death after a couple of hours of fearful suffering.

"The walnuts will be worm-eaten and withered." In 1852, a report sent to the French Ministry of the Interior stated that, the preceding year, a disease had totally destroyed the walnut crop in the regions of Lyon, Beaujolais and Isère. It added that this was a great calamity for the regions in question, since walnuts were one of the mainstays of the local economy.

"The grapes will rot ..." A plague began to attack grapes at this period, as a result of the importation of American vines; it is a century since phylloxera and mildew first began to ravage vineyards.

The punishments announced by Our Blessed Mother as proof of the authenticity of her message were fully confirmed. The apparition took place in 1846, and the newspaper reports that we have mentioned begin with the year 1847 and cover the period ending in 1852. So, the forecasts began to

come true immediately.

The Immaculate Conception (1858)

14.—Between February 11th and July 16th, 1858, the Virgin appeared eighteen times to Bernadette Soubirous, a fourteen year old girl from Lourdes. It is a well-known story. The vision gave her the same message as usual, and insisted that people should do penance. But, at the same time, she acknowledged the proclamation by the Church on December 8th, 1854, of the first glory of Mary, her Immaculate Conception.

We have already seen the origin of the miraculous spring at Lourdes, when Bernadette scooped out some earth at the vision's bidding.

The Cafe France in Lourdes was the meeting place of the intelligentsia who were opposed to such mystical phenomena and everything else to do with religion. On behalf of science, they appointed Dr. Dozous to put an end to this superstitious tomfoolery.

Taking upon himself the role of representative of rational men the world over, men who need to see in order to believe, the doctor made his way to the grotto and approached the child. He felt her pulse. His cronies were hanging on his every word and gesture. But Dr. Dozous kept a prudent silence. The fact was that he could not believe his eyes. That first day, when he returned from the grotto, his only comment was: "I still don't know anything at all. It is not possible to get a clear idea after a single examination. I shall go back again."

And go back he did. When asked whether he had seen anything, another intellectual who had accompanied him, replied without a trace of his flippancy of the eve: "I saw the impressive expression on Bernadette's face".

From close at hand, Dr. Dozous watched in puzzlement as Bernadette moved about at the invisible being's commands. The doctor was impressed by the ease with which the young girl scrambled up the slope on her knees. He watched as she scooped away some soil, and he saw the water burbling irresistibly forth. But there was something else that surprised him even more. This, for him, was decisive proof that there was no natural explanation for what his eyes beheld.

"She was on her knees," said the representative of the world of science, in his description of the scene, "reciting with angelic devoutness the prayers of her rosary, which she was holding in her left hand, while in her right she had a thick, lighted candle. At the moment when she began to climb the slope on her knees as usual, there suddenly came a halt in this movement. Her right hand approached her left, and she placed the flame of the heavy candle beneath the fingers of her left hand which were spread apart so that the flame easily passed between them. A fairly strong breeze got up at that moment, and made the flame flicker, but it did not seem to cause any harm to the skin it touched."

"Astonished at this strange occurrence, I prevented anyone stopping it, and, taking out my pocket-watch, I timed it for a quarter of an hour."

"After this interval, Bernadette, who was still in a state of ecstasy, separated her two hands and advanced to the top of the grotto. In this way the action of the flame on her left hand ceased."

When the child came out of her trance, Dr. Dozous examined her hand, but could find absolutely nothing the matter with it. He then asked her to relight her candle and, taking her hand, he forced it into the flame. The child jumped back sharply, complaining that he had scorched her.

The Blessed Virgin taught the young girl how to make the Sign of the Cross. Many accounts mention the ample, graceful motions with which Bernadette imitated Our Lady, making the Sign of the Cross with the Crucifix on her rosary from the time of the first vision onwards. This act, impressively dignified in so humble and ignorant a child, brought tears to the eyes of all who witnessed it.

Then came the miracles, increasing in numbers from the 5th to the 25th of March. And they have never ceased from that day to this. The most spectacular cures at the time were those of Eugene Oroy of Bareges, Henri Busquet, Denis Bouchet, Croisine Ducoups, etc. But, most important of all were the spiritual cures that packed the churches and confessionals to overflowing. It was in those early days that the first pair of crutches was hung in the grotto, an offering by a paralytic who recovered the use of his leg when it came into contact with the Lourdes water. Since then, the spring has continued to flow, and with it has come an incessant stream of pilgrims.

The medical bureau at Lourdes subjects the most inexplicable of the cures to meticulous study and analysis.

I cannot resist the temptation to include here the personal testimony of the Most Rev. Fr. Arrupe, S.J., who was elected General of the Society of Jesus in May 1965.

In his recollections of life as a missionary in Japan, Fr. Arrupe gives an account of the beginnings of his vocation. While a medical student at the San Carlos Faculty in Madrid, he took the opportunity of spending a month in Lourdes. "I was full of curiosity when I arrived in Lourdes." His was the curiosity of a practising Catholic, but also of an undergraduate in search of the truth, and rather inclined to be skeptical. It did not take him long to reach the conviction that "life in Lourdes is a miracle". Critical in attitude and inclined to be scientifically argumentative, the student was lucky enough to witness the verification of three cases of miracles at the Bureau de Constatation or Medical Records Office. "I had so often heard some of my professors at San Carlos ranting against the mumbo-jumbo at Lourdes ..."[†]

Fr. Arrupe was able to check these miracles himself. Today, he is recognized as an international authority on psychiatric medicine. As he himself writes: "I must admit that those three miracles, of which I myself was a witness, deeply impressed me. After studying my profession in an irreligious university atmosphere where the professors did nothing but launch diatribes against the supernatural on behalf, so they said, of science, I found God three times through three miracles."

[†] Most Rev. Fr. Arrupe, S.J. "Este Japón Increible", PP. 16 to 20

Our Lady of Fatima (1917)

15.—As time went on, the Virgin's apostleship grew more and more spectacular and, consequently, her messages for the world became easier for mankind to believe.

Our Lady put every effort into her mission. She was generous in her intercession, announced exactly where she would next appear, and promised a spectacular miracle so that everybody would believe. These were the circumstances in her apparition at Fatima. The Blessed Virgin promised to return on the 13th of every month for six months in succession. She announced a miracle for noon on October 13th. With the general faith growing gradually weaker, a special helping hand was needed, in the shape of supernatural assistance to raise mankind up to God. So, Our Lady's miracles would have to be more convincing because of Man's greater resistance to faith and, also, perhaps, because the "Cup" of divine justice was gradually filling and the threat of a possible punishment was ever more imminent.

"In October, I shall tell you who I am and what I want of you. And I shall work a miracle which all must see to believe."

The message was fundamentally the same as all her previous ones. She appealed for people to make sacrifices in reparation for sinners; she asked people to say the rosary to obtain peace in the world and an end to the war; she showed the children a vision of Hell, where the souls of impenitent sinners go. To save us. Our Lord wished to establish the devotion to the Immaculate Heart of Mary and the Holy Communion of expiation on the first Saturday of the month . . . "If mankind does as I ask, many souls will be saved and there will be peace. The war (1914-18) is going to end, but, if men do not stop offending the Lord, another worse war will begin under the next pontificate. When you see a night made bright by a great unknown light, be sure that it is the sign sent by God and that the punishment of the world is at hand through war, famine and persecution against the Church and against the Holy Father."

This sign from God in the form of a strange light came on January 25th, 1938. The newspapers of January 26th referred to this surprising event seen all over Europe. It happened between ten and eleven o'clock at night. On the coast of Belgium it was seen as a rainbow; it had a dark red and violet glow. At Briançon, post-office workers were able to work by this aurora without any other illumination. The descriptions of the phenomenon differed from one place to another, but there were many eyewitnesses in different countries.

This is one piece of evidence supporting the apparitions at Fatima.

Another is the attitude adopted by the visionaries when Oliveira Santos, the mayor of Ourem, kidnapped them, locked them in jail and threatened to have them all "fried alive in a great big fryingpan." He led them away, one by one, pretending that he was carrying out his threats. Though fully convinced that they were about to be burnt alive, nevertheless, all three heroically accepted death rather than recant or betray the secret confided to them by Our Lady.

But the principal proof lies in the miracle of the sun, which cannot be refuted however closely it is studied.

History tells us of no similar case: a miracle announced in advance as if it were a public spectacle, even with all the trimmings of prior publicity. From the farthest corners of Portugal and even from abroad, pilgrims came in their thousands to witness the big event. More than seventy thousand people are estimated to have been present on the day. The Liberal Press sent reporters after declaring that, the following day, they would report the end of the farce. But the story was not published in any of the papers with atheistic leanings, except those which, despite their ideology, did not mind publishing the truth and admitting that a truly inexplicable event had taken place.

In utter amazement, the multitude watched the miracle. The sky peeped through as the clouds dispersed. The rain stopped instantly. In the center, like a silver moon, was the orb of the sun. All at once, it began to revolve like a pinwheel, casting forth flashes of multi-hued flames. The dazzling glow of every color in the rainbow, yellows, reds, greens and blues, was reflected on the clouds, trees and hills, a fantastic scene of Nature unleashed by its Maker. Within a few minutes the sun ceased its dance and began to shine with a light that did not dazzle the eyes; then, the crazy whirling was resumed. This prodigy happened three times; and, each time, the dance became wilder and the colors brighter. "And throughout the unforgettable twelve minutes that this breathtaking spectacle lasted, the crowd stood there in gaping suspense, contemplating the overwhelming drama which could be seen for more than 25 miles."

The sun suddenly flew from its place in the firmament and crashed earthwards on top of the crowd. A deafening shriek was wrenched from every throat. Some fell to their knees, some screamed, some prayed . . . When it was near the earth, the sun halted in its tracks and, then, slowly, majestically, it returned to its normal position in the sky. It recovered its usual dazzling brightness. The sky was a clear, cloudless blue. The spectators *en masse* began to recite the Credo. Their clothes, which had been drenched with rain a few moments earlier, had dried out in an instant. The enthusiasm was indescribable. The Blessed Virgin had kept her word, and mankind now had the proof it needed in order to believe. Fr. Federico Gutierrez wrote of Fatima:

"This spectacle was clearly seen three times, in the space of more than ten minutes, by some seventy thousand people, some believers, others unbelievers; some, simple citizens, others men of science. The children had announced the exact day and hour in advance. No astronomical observatory recorded the phenomenon, and this is sufficient proof that it had no natural explanation. Some saw it several miles from the actual spot."[†]

Rumors of the miracle spread like wildfire throughout Portugal and beyond the frontiers. It was reported in the Press all over the world. Lisbon's leading newspaper, *"O'Seculo"*, published long articles under headlines that read: "Amazing events", and "How the Sun Danced at Noon over Fatima". Paulino D'Almeida, head of the editorial staff and a man who had boasted of his incredulity, published an article of his own in *"O'Seculo"* on October 15th, 1917, entitled "In the Midst of the Supernatural". The article read as follows: "And then, we witnessed a unique spectacle, incredible for those who were not there to see it... The sun was like a plaque of tarnished silver. It did not dazzle the eyes! It was as if there had been an eclipse . . . But, all at once, a great clamor arose: 'A miracle, a miracle!' Before the terrified gaze of the pale-faced, bare-headed multitude, whose behavior was reminiscent of Biblical times as they contemplated the blue sky above, the sun started to tremble. It began to move erratically in a way never seen before, in defiance of all cosmic laws. The sun 'started to dance', as the peasants themselves described it ... All we need now is for the experts to explain to us, from their dizzy heights of knowledge, the meaning of the macabre solar dance which today drew cries of 'Hosannah' from the throats of thousands, a sight that reliable sources report as having greatly impressed even the freethinkers, and other people without any religious inclinations at all, who witnessed this historic dance."

The message was fully confirmed. The voice was truly that of Heaven speaking to our generations. It spoke for our benefit, just as it had previously spoken for our grandparents'. But we who are so exacting need more than this to believe, and Heaven gave us further proof. Like so many St. Thomases, Heaven permitted us to see and touch so that we might believe. How difficult it was to become for modern man to visit Fatima, ascertain that it was genuine from all the evidence, and then find an excuse to flee from his faith.

[†] Fr. Federico Gutierrez; "La Verdad sobre Fatima", page 44.

I am sure Monroy[†] cannot have bothered to leaf through the Portuguese newspapers of that day, such a recent date. I do not suppose, either, that he has seen the photographs that exist; all these pieces of evidence are easily found, and would have helped him to investigate the truth; perhaps he would have greater difficulty in finding evidence to substantiate Samuel's appearance to King Saul...

The two little shepherds, Francisco and Jacinta, died within a short time, just as Our Lady had foretold. Their deaths, amid great suffering, gave them both a chance to show the heroic spirit of their souls, desirous to suffer and offer their sufferings for sinners.

But, the most comforting part of all the message comes after Our Lady speaks of the Russian Revolution as a threat and scourge for the entire human race, when she says: "But, in the end, my Immaculate Heart will triumph . .." Perhaps the part of the message that has remained a secret refers to the moment of her triumph, the date when the reign of the Hearts of Jesus and Mary is to begin. However, there is some fear, and indeed there is now evidence to back it, that that moment will come only after a terrible punishment which will uproot the rotten weeds of sin from the face of the earth, like the great flood in Noah's day.

As little Jacinta constantly repeated throughout her illness, the essential part of the message of Fatima is contained in the words which she used in reply to Dr. Formigal the day after the dance of the sun, when he asked the little visionary what Our Lady had said: "I have come to tell you not to offend Our Lord any more, for He has already been offended too much; if people make amends, the war will come to an end; and if they do not make amends, the world will come to an end."

These words bear a marked resemblance to those of the visionaries at San Sebastian de Garabandal.

Syracuse (1953)

16.—This review of the surprising world of the Marian apparitions would not be complete without a short reference to Our Lady of Syracuse, the Virgin who, as at La Salette, manifested her presence to the world by weeping, stricken by the disasters of mankind. The weeping of Our Lady of Syracuse has drawn thousands of fervent pilgrims who go there to mingle their own human tears with those divine ones shed in Syracuse for four consecutive days and seen by the entire population. There were not just a few, more or less chosen people who witnessed this extraordinary case, but a whole city

---

[†] See Appendix

comprised of believers and unbelievers, scholars and ignorant souls, atheists and clergy, millions of people saw the phenomenon during those four days when Our Lady's human tears moved the populace.

The story is a simple one, like all supernatural prodigies. Antonia Giusto, a young working-girl in Syracuse, married Angelo Ianusso when she was twenty. Among their wedding-presents was a simple plaster wall-shrine which had cost about 3,500 lire in a local shop. Antonia and Angelo were poor, as was only too common immediately after the war, and they had difficulty in finding work, let alone a home. However, they settled in temporarily with Angelo's mother and brother. Antonia was expecting a baby. But her pregnancy was further complicated by a series of epileptic fits and pains of all kinds. The poor woman was very depressed and, seeking consolation in her faith, frequently prayed before the plaster Virgin. The doctors diagnosed her complaint as gestational toxicosis, and she was ordered to stay in bed without moving. Her pain grew worse and worse, and although he had not completely lost his faith, her husband Angelo complained of his misfortune. At heart, he scoffed at his wife's prayers.[†]

At 8:30 a.m. on August 29th, 1953, Antonia turned to the image of the Virgin for comfort when her suffering became unbearable. To her astonishment, she saw that the Virgin was weeping. She called to her sister-in-law who, not knowing what to do, evidently decided to treat the Virgin as yet another patient entrusted to her care. She carefully began to wipe the Madonna's sorrowful eyes. This done, she summoned the rest of the family.

Meanwhile, Antonia's pains had vanished. She got out of bed and devoted her whole attention to the Virgin's weeping. For some hours, she simply watched the miracle and used handkerchiefs and then pieces of cotton-batting to wipe Our Lady's abundant tears away. Finally, the women came to the conclusion that something had to be done. At someone's suggestion, they called the police. Skeptical and amused, the police arrived on the scene and were taken aback to find that the Virgin really was weeping . . .

By the time Antonia's husband returned home, the house was crowded with people. The local police commissioner, *Chief* Ferrigmo, came to see for himself. Not knowing what steps to take, he removed the image to the police station. Our Lady continued weeping all the way. The jeep was bathed in her tears, which trickled to the ground. It was 9 p.m., Saturday the 29th of August. The Blessed Virgin had been crying almost all day long.

[†] Estigmatizados y Apariciones", page 192 onwards.

When they reached the police station, the tears ceased. The officers of the law were at a loss as to what to do with the little shrine, and finally elected to return it to its owner. But, Angelo was frightened to go home to the crowds. Then, he tucked it under his arm and vanished into the night, as if guilty of a crime, trudging from house to house to avoid the crowds who were anxious to see the prodigy at all costs. But the public were not to be placated, and the rumor spread that Our Lady had been arrested by the police. Infuriated at the very idea, they fell upon Angelo's brother, who fled. At midnight, the fugitive Angelo returned furtively home bearing his plaster shrine, which he deposited on some cushions. Mary was weeping again . . .

Next day, Sunday August 30th, a multitude gathered before the house at an early hour. Many had even spent the night there. Police magistrate Nicolas Samperisi came to the scene to calm the crowds. He entered the bedroom and watched the scene. The shrine with the Madonna was propped up on the bed, tears trickling down her cheeks. The impatient crowd were raising a tumult in the street below. The shrine was placed on a little table, and a line was organized so that the public could see the miracle for themselves. The first priest to see it was Fr. Vicenzo Sapio, chaplain of Syracuse General Hospital. The news had spread, not only to the farthest corners of Syracuse, but throughout Sicily. From all parts of the island people came in droves by car, taxi, bus . . . The line still jammed the street. It was first decided to display the Madonna on the balcony overlooking the street, but it was eventually hung on the wall of a house opposite, belonging to Prof. Lucea, who owned a small front garden protected by a wall. A temporary altar was built and, there, the miraculous statue was installed. And now, there commenced a personal dialogue between the people and their Madonna. The rosary was recited aloud. Graces and favors were implored ... At 11 p.m on Tuesday September 1st, the tears stopped. The pieces of cotton-batting drenched in those divine, yet human, bitter salty tears were distributed through Syracuse and then all over the world. The prodigy was witnessed by people from every walk of life. The Virgin chose a little shrine in the home of a poor working-class family and wept for nearly four days with very few, brief respites. Today, her tears are working wonders on the bodies and souls of undeserving humanity. Antonia never experienced any further pain, and her child was born normally, little knowing that he had been the indirect cause of the Mother of God's tears.

A few days afterwards, letters and telegrams started to arrive from all over the world, addressed to "The Weeping Virgin" or

"The Madonna of the Tears". The post-office employees heaped them at the foot of the shrine. Photographs had been taken and were handed round. Experts and men of science gave evidence. One such testimony reads as follows: "With the assistance of the police, who made way for us through the immense crowds in front of the house, we entered a bedroom with a single window giving onto the Via Carso. There, at our request, Signora Antonia Giusto unlocked a box in which, wrapped in a piece of linen, there lay an image of the Blessed Virgin which appeared to be made of plaster in different colors, backed by a sheet of black glass."

"The image undoubtedly showed signs of humidity on various parts of the face and chest, but the liquid had been carefully wiped off with pieces of cotton-wool. Only a single drop remained in the corner of the left eye. The said drop was removed with the help of a pipette. One after another, several drops welled up in the same place and were likewise collected.

"While the drops were being transferred to a glass tube, some more tears sprang from the eye and trickled down to the little hollow formed by the hand holding the heart of the Virgin. These tear drops were also collected.

"In the course of these operations, we could not prevent the onlookers from soaking up some tears with pieces of cotton-batting. Altogether, a little more than one cubic centimeter of liquid was removed to the laboratory.

"The phenomenon lasted almost a quarter of an hour from the time the image was taken from the box, and it did not occur again, so it was not possible to obtain any more material for the analysis.

"The inner corners of the eyes were examined with magnifying glasses, hut no pores or flaws could be seen in the ceramic surface. The plaster image was separated from its black glass backing, and it was observed to be made of a block of plaster from one to two centimeters in thickness.

"The outer part was varnished in several different colors, and the unworked inner face had a smooth white surface which proved to be quite dry on examination."

This testimonial was signed by three doctors and the parish priest, Fr. Giuseppe Bruno.

The original report on the analysis of the liquid is too lengthy to be given here in full, but it ends with the following findings:

"In brief, its appearance, its alkali content and composition indicate that the liquid examined has a composition analogous to that of the human lacrimal secretion.

Syracuse, September 9th, 1953.

Signed: Dr. Michele Cassola, Director of the Micrographic Section of the Provincial Laboratory.

Dr. Francesco Cotzia, Assistant Director of the Micrographic Section of the Syracuse Provincial Laboratory.

Dr. Leopoldo La Rosa, Chemist of the Department of Hygiene.

Dr. Mario Marletta, Surgeon.

The undersigned parish priest, Fr. Giuseppe Bruno, hereby declares that he was present during the examination of the liquid mentioned in this report, and that he received from the signatories of same a solemn oath taken on the Gospels, the said signatories having signed this document in his presence. (Sgnd.) Giuseppe Bruno."

From the moment when the tears first started to trickle down Our Lady's cheeks, graces and favors began to be granted to many who asked for them. Many prodigies took place in other countries, far from Syracuse, when people touched pieces of cotton-batting that had not even been used to wipe the Virgin's tears away, but had merely been brushed over the dry face of the image. A typical example is that of young Benita Juarez, a pupil at the Santa Maria School for the Blind, run by the Theresian Sisters at Villalba, Spain. Benita recovered her sight when her eyes touched a scrap of cotton sent from Syracuse. Mariano Sastre, aged eighteen, who lives in the suburbs of Madrid, was cured instantly of the paralysis that had crippled him since boyhood. Many are the cases of this type to prove the authenticity of this prodigy which has been granted Church approval.

The Virgin of Syracuse with her silent weeping was a resumption of the messages of La Salette, Lourdes and Fatima, as the Mother of God grows increasingly sorrowful at human conduct, and fearful of not being able to restrain much longer her Son's justice, which demands a punishment as an example. As Senator Luigi Sturzo says, "Perhaps that is why Our Blessed Mother weeps; She does so because men put themselves in the hands of the powers of destruction instead of construction; they prefer hatred to love, envy to concord, pride of race, caste or class to brotherhood and international cooperation. The Virgin weeps because the world does not pray; and the world does not know how to pray because it is rotten with pride and does now bow its head to God or invoke the Holy Spirit. The world believes and trusts in men; it does not believe, and consequently does not trust, in God."

Now the question mark:

17.—From this brief review of Our Lady's main apparitions, we can pick out a series of circumstances that are common to them all. The same circumstances are also in evidence at San Sebastian de Garabandal, and it is this that leads us to conclude that the happenings at the little upland village may quite well take their place someday as a continuation of the logical, natural evolution of the Marian apparitions.

The matter has attracted the attention of prestigious devout associations, of authors, of specialists mainly from abroad, all of whom have followed the story of Garabandal closely and have publicized the principal events in circulars, newspaper articles and leaflets.

In Spain itself, the matter has not received the publicity it deserves, doubtless as a result of the notes published by the bishop of Santander on August 26th and October 24th, 1961. These notes stated that, *for the moment* there was no positive proof of the supernatural origin of the occurrences, and forbade priests to go to the village without the bishop's express permission, recommending the public to refrain from taking active part in a series of events on which clarification was still pending.

However, the altitude of justified prudence on the Church's part, adopted by the bishop of Santander—an attitude which is altogether praiseworthy—is, I think, compatible with an objective and truthful exposition of the facts in the manner of a mere report. And, I feel this is particularly true when a book has been published containing grave distortions of these facts.

As a certain leaflet printed in French so rightly says, "if, in recent days, the Mother of God has appeared five times in France, Portugal, Belgium and Italy, what is there to prevent her paying one of her merciful visits to Spain . . . ?" After all, Spain is a country of proven Christian mettle and Marian devotion.

What does stand out after a study of the question is that neither at Fatima, nor at Lourdes, Syracuse, Paris, Banneux, Pontmain, or anywhere else, for that matter, has the assumed Vision had such a wealth of spectacular attendant phenomena. In no previous case have the apparitions been so frequent or lasted so long. It is almost as if all the prodigies in the history of mysticism had made a rendezvous at Garabandal. Continual raptures, supernatural locutions, ecstatic falls and walks, cases of levitation, Holy Communion administered by an Angel—the Holy Eucharist being visible in one case when the miracle was duly announced in advance by the visionary—colloquies, etc. And, to cap it all, the announcement of a future public miracle, together with some details of the circumstances in which it will take place . . . For the Garabandal story is far from ended . . .

What IS Happening at Garabandal?

Map of Spain, showing the location of Garabandal.

The long climb to Garabandal.

Chapter Two

THE STORY BEGINS

Panoramic view of the village of Garabandal

18.—San Sebastian de Garabandal is a little village of barely seventy homes, nestling on a mountainside. To get there, you have to make a stiff climb along a spur starting at Cosio, where the road, as such, ends. It lies in the province of Santander, some fifty-five miles from the city of Santander itself. The houses are quaint, and the lanes picturesque, though surfaced in rough stone and more often than not deep in mud. San Sebastian de Garabandal is hidden in the heart of the Cantabrian Mountains, at a height of about two thousand feet. The atmosphere is tranquil with its deep silence and undisturbed peace.

Here, isolated from the outside world, live four young girls of humble birth. Their names are Mary Loli, Conchita, Jacinta and Mary Cruz. Mary Loli's surname is Mazon. The other three are all surnamed Gonzalez, although there is no close relationship between them. On June 18th, 1961, Mary Cruz was at the time eleven years old, while the other three were twelve.

It was a Sunday. The parish priest from Cosio, Fr. Valentin Marichalar, had plodded up to San Sebastian to celebrate Mass, as was his custom on Sundays and holidays. After Mass, the villagers usually gathered in the little village square. The children used to go there to play. Like the conversation of the adults, the games played by the little girls had about them the spontaneous simplicity so common in a hamlet like Garabandal, where there is seldom much to discuss. At Garabandal, there are no cafés, bars or entertainment. *"Nothing worth mentioning ever happened"* at Garabandal. Adult talk was of cattle, the state of the pastures, and whether or not it would rain.

But, that afternoon of the 18th of June, Conchita whispered a suggestion for a daring escapade in Mary Cruz's ear. For fun, she proposed that they should slip out of the square, jump over a certain stone wall and scrounge some apples. The apple tree in question stood in a small vegetable patch adjoining the schoolmaster's house. A low wall separated the small plot from the lane leading uphill to the pine grove overlooking the village. They edged their way round the corner, making sure nobody was looking, and made for the object of their prank, the apple tree. But, Mary Loli, Jacinta and another younger child had spotted them both slipping away, and had stealthily followed not far behind. Conchita and Mary Cruz were busily picking apples when the others suddenly appeared on the scene.

Loli	Jacinta	Maria-Cruz	Conchita (1961)
age 12	age 12	age 11	age 12

"Conchita, you're stealing apples," Jacinta shouted.

"Hush! Be quiet," hissed Conchita. "If the teacher hears you, she'll tell Mommy."

Frightened lest someone should come to see what was going on, she crouched low and hid in the undergrowth. Mary Cruz, for her part, was in full flight across the fields.

"Don't run away, Mary Cruz," cried Mary Loli. "We've seen you and we're going to tell the owner."

Mary Cruz stopped running and woefully retraced her steps to join her friends. Conchita emerged from her hiding-place. A voice summoned the little girl who had accompanied Jacinta and Mary Loli, and the four older girls were at last alone. For a few moments, they did not know what to do. But, eventually, as Conchita recounts in her diary, "thinking better of it, all four of us went back to picking apples."

They were engrossed in their innocent mischief when they suddenly heard the schoolmaster speaking to his wife. "Go and take a look out in the vegetable patch, and scare away the bees. They're at the apple tree again."

Hearing this, the four girls burst into fits of giggles and, their pockets stuffed with fruit, they scrambled over the wall. They had enjoyed themselves. Panting, they reached the lane and began to munch their booty in peace. Thunder rolled through the mountains.

It was half-past eight in the evening

"Did you hear that?"

"Yes, thunder. It's going to rain."

After satisfying their appetites, they began to feel the first pangs of remorse.

"What we've done isn't right," said one.

"Our guardian angels must be very sad," commented another.

"And the devil must be very pleased," added a third.

It was more or less in these terms that they interpreted what they had heard the parish priest say in catechism class. To repair the harm they had done, Conchita had another idea.

"Let's throw stones at the wicked angel, so as to console the good angel," said she. And picking up some stones from the lane, they began to cast them "to the left, with all our might," says Conchita, "at a spot where we said the devil was." Having thus set their uneasy consciences at rest and shown their repentance, they sat down in the lane to play marbles with some

They sat down in the lane to play marbles.

pebbles. There the four of them were sitting, in the positions seen in the photograph taken shortly afterwards, when, all at once, Conchita saw "a very beautiful figure appear, surrounded by a great light that did not dazzle my eyes."[†] When her three companions saw her transfigured, they imagined that she had had an attack, and they were about to shout for help. But, her hands clasped together, Conchita pointed to the apparition. "Look! Over there!"

Mary Loli had already risen to her feet to fetch help, but now they looked in the direction which Conchita was indicating.

"The angel . . . !" they all gasped. A short silence ensued as the overawed children contemplated the vision before them. They did not say a word. Nor did the angel. Then, he vanished into thin air ...

Interior of the Church
at Garabandal

Very frightened by what they had just seen, they ran to the church. On the way, they passed through the little square where some of the villagers were dancing to the strains of a bagpipe and drum. Here, they ran into a little girl called Pili Gonzalez.

"How pale and scared you all look," Pili remarked. "Where have you been?"

"Stealing apples," they answered, ashamed at having to admit the truth.

"Oh, is that all?" the other rejoined disdainfully.

"We've seen an angel," they chorused.

"D'you really mean it?

"Yes, yes . . . ," they insisted, and hurried off to the church. Meanwhile, the surprised Pili told everybody in the square what she had just heard.

---

† Quoted from Conchita's diary.

34

The Church, seen from the outside.

On arriving at the church, they did not dare enter. The four made their way round to the rear of the building, where they huddled in a corner and started to cry. Some other smaller children were playing nearby and soon discovered them.

"Why are you all crying," they inquired.

" 'Cos we've seen an angel."

The little newcomers ran off to tell the schoolmistress. The four girls felt better for their quiet weeping. Returning to the front of the building, they entered the church. It was not long before the schoolmistress appeared, wearing a look of anxiety and not a little surprised.

"Is it really true that you've seen an angel?"

"Yes, *Señora*"

"It can't have been your imagination, can it?"

"No. We're quite positive we saw him."

"What did he look like?"

"He was wearing a long, seamless blue robe. He had fairly big pink wings. His face was small; it wasn't long and it wasn't round either. His eyes were black. He had fine hands and short finger-nails. His feet weren't in sight. He looked about nine years old. But, although he was a child to look at, he gave the impression of being very strong . . ."

The details gradually came out, one by one. All the girls' replies agreed. The schoolmistress, who had a high opinion of the children, did not doubt their sincerity for a moment.

"In thanksgiving," she said, "let's say a decade of the rosary to the Blessed Sacrament."

This concluded, they made their way home, each filled with a sweet sensation between fear and joy. It was nine o'clock.

Señora Gonzalez, who doted on her daughter, greeted Conchita with ill-humor.

"A fine time of night to be coming home! Haven't I told you many a time, you're to be back before dark?"

Still spellbound by her recollection of that glowing figure, and disconcerted by her mother's reproaches for arriving so late, Conchita did not dare enter the ground-floor kitchen where the household spent much of the time. She leant awkwardly against the passage wall near the outer door.

"You see, Mother," she began, "we saw an angel today."

"So!" retorted Señora Gonzalez indignantly. "On top of coming home late, you're going to tell me a lot of nonsense."

"No, Mother, honestly. We did see an angel."

Such insistence left Aniceta Gonzalez nonplussed. She knew that her daughter was customarily truthful. Tentatively at first, Conchita started to tell her mother what had occurred. She ventured some more details. Senora Gonzalez was at a loss, but decided that silence was the best policy.

"Go on up to bed. We'll discuss it in the morning." It was a quarter past nine.

Conchita's house.

The First Trials

19.—Next day, Monday June 19th, the news had spread round the village like wildfire.

"What would an angel want to come to San Sebastian for?"

"I expect they were suffering from hallucinations. But, they must have seen something, because they looked really frightened."

"I noticed they looked rather pale and seemed to be trembling."

"They sat there crying for quite a while."

"Their descriptions matched when they gave details of the figure they saw."

"They say he had wings."

"It must have been one of those big birds."

"More likely some little child. It was almost dark."

The whole village was agog with the news. The questions rained thick and fast. The little girls answered one villager after another without hesitation. They gave a more detailed description of the angel's appearance and the strange glow that enveloped him.

Amid more or less mocking questions and remarks, they went to school. It was ten o'clock. Before starting the morning's classes, the schoolmistress asked them the same question as the night before.

"Children, are you sure of what you said yesterday?"

"*Si, Señora.* Yes, we are." And they told their story, to the admiration of their schoolmates, who plied them with eager questions. Classes began. "We did everything just as usual," writes Conchita in her diary, "without worrying any more about it."

At one o'clock, classes ended and they went home. Jacinta and Mary Cruz were walking along together when they were overtaken by the parish priest from Cosio.

"What's all this I hear? Did you really see the angel?"

"Yes, Father."

"I'm not too sure, myself . . . Perhaps your eyes played tricks on you."

"Honestly, we weren't mistaken," they answered, smiling. "We saw the angel."

They proceeded on their way. Fr. Valentin turned his steps towards Conchita's house.

Halfway there, he met the child. Conchita recalls that the priest looked agitated.

"Come now," he said. "Tell me the whole truth. What did you see last night?"

Conchita told him the story, taking care not to omit any details. Don Valentin listened attentively.

"Well," he instructed her as they parted, "if you see him again this evening, ask him who he is and what he is after."

Fr. Marichalar now made for Mary Loli's house to complete his inquiries. He was astonished to discover that her replies were identical.

"We'll wait a day or so," the priest puckered his brow, "to see if this beautiful person returns, and see what he has to say. Then, I'll go in to Santander and have a word with the Bishop."

The girls had their lunch and returned to their afternoon lessons. Afterwards, Conchita went to buy some milk. The woman who sold it to her, a friend of Señora Gonzalez, questioned her afresh. Conchita relates that, after hearing her out, the woman smiled kindly.

"Since I know you well," she commented, "I believe you saw the angel. But not the others."

"That isn't so. We were together, all four of us, and we all saw him quite plainly."

She carried the milk home and asked her mother's permission to go to the sunken lane to pray. The house was undergoing repairs. Pepe Diez and Conchita's brother, Aniceto Gonzalez, were working there. Pepe smiled when he heard her request.

"Let her go," he said to her mother. "She can't do anyone any harm by praying!"

"Not on your life, Mother," Aniceto broke in. "Do you want us all to be a laughing stock?"

They were in the midst of this when the other three girls came round the corner. Aniceta was in a quandary. She wanted to let Conchita have her way, but she would have liked to have heeded Aniceto's sensible advice, too.

"Oh Lord!" she exclaimed. "What a fix they've got us into!"

"It isn't a fix, Mother," Conchita put in.

"And what if it's all true? !" Aniceta mused.

She finally gave her consent, and the four set off happily for the lane leading to the pine grove and the spot called the *"calleja"* or sunken lane; their own "little piece of heaven," as it is called in the diary.

"Where are you off to?" people inquired as they passed by.

"To pray in the lane."

"What on earth are you going to the lane for? Haven't you got a perfectly good church to pray in?"

"Yesterday, we saw the angel there, so now we're going to pray and see if he appears there again." Followed by the neighbors' smiles and jokes, the girls went on. When they reached the spot where they had been the night before, they knelt down. Passers-by in the lane and some little boys and girls who had followed them laughed heartily. They attempted to force the girls to leave the lane.

Typical houses of Garabandal.

A group of youngsters decided to use a more persuasive argument. Crouching hidden among the maize-stalks in a field above the sunken lane, they started to throw stones. Jacinta, Mary Loli, Conchita and Mary Cruz protested, and begged to be left in peace to say the rosary.

The sky was overcast, and a strong wind was blowing. Perhaps the behavior of the rascals in the maize field was the reason why there was no apparition that afternoon. A place that is in the process of being stoned is hardly the most auspicious spot for the enormous grace of a heavenly vision.

Night fell. Accompanied by the jeers of everyone about them, they went to the church to say a decade to the Blessed Sacrament. The schoolmistress met them on the way.

"Have you been up the lane?"

"Yes, we have. But we didn't see anything."

"Don't worry," the teacher reassured them. The children's disappointment at that moment only convinced her the more of the vision of the previous night. "Don't worry, He'll come tomorrow."

"Why didn't he come today?" they asked.

"Most likely because it has been clouded over."

It was a quarter past six when they entered the church. Afterwards they went home.

"Well? Did you see the angel?" their families asked.

"No, we didn't see anyone today."

They settled down to do their homework, had supper and went to bed. "It must have been a quarter to ten," Conchita recalls, "when I started to say my prayers. And then, we each heard a voice that said: 'Do not worry. You will see me again'. "The phenomenon happened to all four girls at the same time, each in her respective home. Frightened at this strange occurrence, "we went on fervently saying our prayers until we fell asleep."[†]

The site of many apparitions:
the Sunken Lane leading to the Pines (top).

[†] From Conchita's diary.

The Visions' Light

20.—The locution is another common phenomenon in the annals of the mystics. In the apparitions of the Blessed Virgin, it generally occurs when the visions come to an end, as a means of continuing the contact between the Virgin and her visionaries. As we saw in the previous chapter, the Vision said to Sister Catherine Labouré: "You will not see me again, but you will hear my voice in your prayers." This has been particularly frequent in the case of Lucy of Fatima. We shall see in due course how, at Garabandal, these locutions came to replace the direct colloquies with the Vision. The "llamadas" or calls, which we shall also deal with, described by the visionaries as a sort of unspoken inner summons, likewise fall within this category of mystical phenomena.

On the 20th, in their kitchen, Conchita again had difficulty in obtaining her mother's permission to return to the lane. She was still trying to persuade her to change her mind when the other three arrived.

"You three go," Conchita's mother was firm. "Conchita is staying home." Reluctantly they departed, but they dawdled just round the corner. Conchita was crestfallen. Going to the door, Señora Gonzalez hailed Mary Loli.

"Come here, the three of you. Now, listen. If you do as I tell you, I'll let Conchita go with you."

Overjoyed at this, they agreed. Aniceta had a plan. She had devised a neat ruse so that her daughter could go, but at the same time be saved from ridicule.

"You go on ahead as if you were going to play, without breathing a word to a soul. When you reach the lane, Conchita will creep round to join you, across the fields."

They were none too sure that Aniceta would keep her word. They looked dubious as they left.

"You run on ahead," Conchita reassured them, "I'll be right behind you."

Outside the village, Conchita caught up with them. Happy and excited, the four companions came to their usual spot and knelt down to pray. They finished saying the rosary, and still the angel did not appear.

"We were just getting to our feet to start back to the village," says Conchita, "when we saw a shining light blocking the path." Blinded by the light, the startled children were disconcerted and afraid. Conchita records in her diary that they "gave a scream of horror". But the light soon dimmed. They recovered their vision of all about them, and set off down the lane towards the village church. The angel was preparing the girls for their heavenly visions. This is why, first of all, they saw his figure and, later, the bright light that accompanied the visions. So it was to go on until he had prepared them to enter and leave with amazing frequency that gorgeous stage where celestial beings appeared, spoke and moved.

They began to feel themselves more a part of heaven than of earth. At first, they did not tell anyone about their experience of that day. Realizing that others would not understand, they were silent and kept these wonders to themselves. But, next day, they remembered the parish priest's admonishment. "If you see anything again, don't fail to let me know at once."

They had to tell Fr. Valentin Marichalar about the light, but their parents would not allow them to descend the mountain to Cosio. In the end, they saw that there was no other alternative but to tell their parents everything, so that the latter could speak to the priest. Their parents did as they asked. The news spread. "But, now," says Conchita, "people were beginning to believe a little."

The Angel Returns

21.—It was the 21st of June. The children felt they had their families' blessings. That afternoon, Aniceta needed no persuading to let her daughter go. Something, however, told the four that they should not go alone. They asked a neighbor, Señora Clementina Gonzalez, to accompany them. At first, Clementina did not dare accept the invitation. Besides, she did not believe any of their tales. She called on a friend and asked her advice. How about them both going along? The women decided that no harm could come of it if there were two of them. They would accompany the children just to satisfy their feminine curiosity. Clementina Gonzalez and her friend Concesa joined the little group of girls. As they proceeded up the path, they passed several neighbors. Seeing the children accompanied by two adults, the neighbors did not hesitate to join the party, too.

So it happened that several villagers were there to say the rosary that afternoon of June 21st. One of the girls led the mysteries, while the rest gave the responses. They said the five decades, but nothing happened. The first smothered laughter was heard, the first wisecracks.

"Let's say another decade, and see if that way ..."

They said another decade amid a certain amount of sniggering. Then, as they ended the decade, all at once the extraordinary thing happened. As one, the four girls seemed suddenly to be frozen to the spot. Kneeling there, they wore a sweet expression on their
pale faces, which seemed to reflect a strange light. All four were looking in

42

the same direction, absorbed. Their heads were thrown back at a surprising angle. Their unblinking eyes were staring up at the heavens. One smiled. Another posed the question that the parish priest had instructed them to ask.

"Who are you? Why have you come?" But the angel did not answer. The laughter and chuckles had ceased. The onlookers were gripped by a sudden fear of the supernatural. Her nerves on edge, Clementina started to cry.

"It's true, it's true. An angel really has appeared to these little ones."

As suddenly as they entered their rapture, the four emerged from it, quite normal and smiling. They looked very happy. The heavenly visit left them an aftermath of inner sweetness. People gathered round, hugging and kissing them. The news was around the village in no time. Knots of people formed to discuss it. The strangest theories were ventured as to the cause of the prodigy.

"If you don't believe this, it's because you don't believe in God," said the most enthusiastic villagers.

The children were continually beset with questions. "People were overcome," Conchita describes the scene, "because they had never seen or heard the likes of it before."

But, what would an angel want to descend from heaven to Garabandal for?

Divine Sleep

22.—The parish priest at Cosio heard all about the happenings of the previous evening from several sources. He was impatient to report to his superiors. Some prudent souls, however, advised him to wait until the following day, since he would then be able to see for himself and give the bishop a first-hand account.

He accepted this sound advice and, that evening, at a quarter past eight, he was on hand with a group of neighbors. Together, they said the rosary and, the very instant they finished, the girls went into a state of ecstasy. Among the onlookers was a teacher called Manin . . .[†] Throughout the rapture, the visionaries were impervious to pain, pin-pricks and burns. It was as if they were deep in a divine slumber; they were unaware of anything that occurred about them. They entered a field of vision placed above the natural plane, a state that isolated them from the things of this world. When they were in an ecstasy, they could see each other.

[†] The first suspicions of possible hypnotic influence fell upon this teacher. He was consequently obliged to leave the scene of the apparitions.

L. to R.: Loli, Conchita, Jacinta, and Maria-Cruz in ecstasy photographed in July 1961

But, if one of them lost her state of ecstasy, she disappeared from the field of vision of the others, as though the rapture were a stage and one of the visionaries had gone off into the wings. Their insensitivity to pain seems to have been complete. Tests were made, such as pricking them hard, but they brought no reaction whatsoever. When they suddenly fell to their knees, they crashed to the ground with tremendous force, but showed not the slightest sign of pain. One totally reliable eye-witness was deeply impressed on one occasion, when Mary Loli fell and hit her head on the edge of a step. The step in question was made of cement. The noise of the jarring blow was spine-chilling. "The bystanders", says the eyewitness, "smothered a scream of horror, but the child remained calmly sitting on the floor, smiling and chatting happily with the Virgin. When she came out of her, rapture, they asked whether she had felt the blow. She could recall nothing. She said that it had perhaps been the cause of a sensation which she noticed at one point, like painless pins and needles, all over. On examination, however, her head was seen to have a large bump where it had struck the step."

In other words, when the visionary was in a state of total ecstasy, she was absolutely impervious to pain.

"The most painful pin-pricks, the roughest shaking, even burns and so on, are quite incapable of arousing them from their rapture. Their eyes often move, but only in order to follow the divine vision with a vivacity that seems to enlarge them considerably. They do not perceive any material contact at all, as can be ascertained by

44

quickly passing a light or some other object close in front of their eyes; this does not cause the slightest flicker of their eyelids or pupils."[†]

A film was taken of the visionaries of Garabandal, with the help of powerful spotlights. In a state of ecstasy, the girls came into the blinding light without so much as blinking. When the vision ended and they recovered their normal state, they immediately shut their eyes. Dazzled, they protested at the glare of the lights trained on them. Their reaction can be seen quite clearly in the film.

Loli, Conchita, Jacinta and Maria-Cruz in ecstasy, July 1961.

The light enveloping the visions was very strong. But, unlike ordinary light, it did not hurt the eyes. This explains the reaction of the visionaries to spotlights. On the other hand, when the ecstasy took place at night, in the pine-grove or in the streets where there were no lights, when the girls came to, they were astonished to discover that it was dark. The light enveloping the visions had been as bright as daylight.

When they left on June 22nd, the parish priest and his companions were convinced that the children's ecstatic trances were genuine. It was quite impossible for ignorant little girls eleven and twelve years of age to make such a pretense. The phenomena were beyond any natural explanation. Garabandal had an inexplicable prodigy on its hands. They did not know whether the causes were supernatural or preternatural. But those four children certainly saw and

---

[†] Taken from a complete report drawn up by Fr. Ramon Andreu, on orders from his superiors.

45

spoke to someone. And, to have this vision and dialogue, they underwent a physical change that snatched them from this world and anaesthetized their bodies to natural stimuli of any kind.

From June 23rd to July 1st

23.—On the 23rd, a larger number of spectators accompanied the girls when they went to the lane as usual. The news had spread to the surrounding hamlets. Promptly, at a quarter to nine, the angel appeared. The onlookers watched the scene, their mouths agape. Afterwards, they crowded round to kiss the little girls and ply them with messages to communicate to Heaven. The Civil Guards, the Spanish country police, escorted them to the sacristy where the parish priest wanted to interrogate them. Eventually, Fr. Marichalar emerged from the sacristy. "I have questioned them together and singly," he proclaimed to those waiting at the church door. "All four coincide in their statements. These children undoubtedly see something that is not of this world. It might well be God's work ..."

The crowd dispersed, satisfied at these first impressions.

The following day, June 24th, was a Saturday. From the early afternoon onwards, people began to arrive from distant villages where the news had spread. On the scene of the apparitions, a small barrier had been erected to protect the children from the avalanche of eager spectators. The expectation knew no bounds. "That day," says Conchita, "the Vision did not give us time to start the rosary."

No sooner had they reached the spot than the light appeared, and in its midst stood the angel. Beneath him were some letters and Roman numerals. They asked him the meaning of these, but the angel smiled without saying anything.

When the rapture ended, they were taken in a cart to the church. There, they went into the sacristy one by one to tell Fr. Marichalar what they had seen. But they had not taken sufficient notice of the writing, and none of them could give the priest the explanation he desired.

Next day, Sunday, the crowd was larger than ever. Among the spectators were five priests and several doctors. One doctor took hold of Conchita and lifted her up in the air. But, that strange extra weight that often overcame the girls when in ecstasy caused him to drop her to the ground from a considerable height. A loud crunch was heard as her rigid knees smashed to the stony ground. Conchita's eldest brother, Serafin, attempted to break her fall, but was unable to. He asserts that an inner force checked him.

Afterwards, several spectators drew near to examine the girls' legs. They bore the marks of the pin-pricks, blows, scratches and

46

other signs. In the course of the trance, however, as Conchita herself states, they did not hurt them at all. "They only left marks."[†]

There was no apparition on Monday 26th. The following Tuesday and Wednesday, the visions of the angel were repeated. On the Thursday and Friday, there were no visions either. The total absence of prodigies disheartened many people who had made the climb to Garabandal in the hope of seeing something briefly while they were there.

On Saturday July 1st, there was a great gathering, including many doctors, priests and people from every walk of life. The apparition occurred very early, at half-past seven in the evening. It was still daylight. The vision lasted two hours, which seemed a mere two minutes to the visionaries. The angel spoke. He told them that, next day, Sunday, the Blessed Virgin would come. As at Fatima, visionaries were prepared for their heavenly visitor by the presence of an angel. In Portugal, he said he was the Angel of Peace. At Garabandal, he was St. Michael the Archangel.

The girls asked him the meaning of the writing and the Roman numerals. He told them that the Blessed Virgin would explain it to them. She would appear under the name of Our Lady of Mount Carmel. . .

Conchita recalls that he spoke to them of many things that day. Some of the children's questions made him smile. He departed assuring them that he would return next day to accompany the Virgin.

People from all parts flocked to the village. Expectation had reached a climax.

What would the morrow bring?

Loli, Conchita and Jacinta in ecstasy.

[†] Quoted from Conchita's diary.

    Our Lady of Mount Carmel: 900 years before Christ, the Prophet Elias retired to Mount Carmel (the name means "a Garden") to seek God in solitude. His example was followed by many hermits and thus a religious order originated. After Christianity was brought to the holy men of Mt. Carmel by the Apostles, they preached devotion to the Blessed Virgin Mary, adopting the name of Brothers of Our Lady of Mount Carmel. During the Crusades they fled the Saracens and established themselves precariously in Europe. There in 1251, St. Simon Stock praying for the survival of his community in England had a vision of Our Lady giving him a Scapular (her mantle), as the symbol of her protection.—Ed.

Chapter Three

OUR LADY OF MOUNT CARMEL

24.—Mass on Sunday, July 2nd, was celebrated with great solemnity. The rosary was said in the little church at three o'clock in the afternoon. Afterwards, the girls took the trail path down to Cosio to meet Conchita's brothers who had been away. Halfway to Cosio, they were obliged to turn back. The crowds trudging their way up to San Sebastian de Garabandal recognized the children from photographs and would not allow them to proceed. Some brought them rosaries; others gave them candy; some had come to take souvenir pictures. But, most had come to bombard them with not always discreet questions. A youth from San Sebastian de Garabandal was already riding down on horseback to search for them, when they were offered a ride by the driver of a Land Rover that happened to be passing.

On arrival, they found the few streets jammed with strangers. Among them were eleven priests and several doctors. Just before six o'clock, with the multitude behind them, they set off for the *"cuadro,"* the rude stone enclosure erected on the spot where the angel had appeared in order to prevent the children being crushed by the crowds. They had not reached the spot when; all at once, they found themselves in the presence of the Blessed Virgin. She was accompanied by two angels. One was a stranger; the other was St. Michael. Both wore the same garb. Conchita declares that they were very alike, "as if they were twins". On the Virgin's right, they could see a square of red fire framing a triangle with an eye and some writing. The lettering was in an odd oriental script. This bright square was taken by some to be a symbol of the concept of God.

The visionaries spoke to the Vision at considerable length. Their conversation was extraordinarily natural. "We told her," says Conchita, "that everyone was behind with the hay-making, and still had the grass piled waiting to be spread to dry. And she laughed at the things we told her."[†]

[†] Quoted from Conchita's diary.

There were two salient points in this conversation. One was the identity of St. Michael the Archangel, which gave rise to a naive remark by one of the children: "I've got a brother called Michael, too, but without the Saint". This brought delighted giggles from her three companions. The second matter was connected with the first revelation of what was later to be the Virgin's message.

All the evidence points to the fact that they received the message in the course of several visions, and not just verbally. In certain respects, they saw it enacted. The sentence: "The Cup is already filling", an expression well-known in Marian terminology, was seen in plastic form. They were shown a large chalice, into which were falling drops of blood or tears. Actually, the children had no idea of the contents of the chalice.

When Our Lady spoke to them of this and of the punishment, she looked very grave. "We have never again seen her looking so sad," says Conchita, "and when pronouncing the words 'The Cup is already filling', she spoke in a very low voice."

The Virgin taught them to say the rosary slowly. At first, she accompanied them herself, but once they knew it properly, She only joined in the "Glory be to the Father."

It was a moving experience, first to hear the little girls praying normally, which they did rather fast, and afterwards to compare it with the same prayer said in ecstasy. Then, the pronunciation was far slower and had an impressive rhythm. There are several copies of tapes in existence on which people managed to record the visionaries' prayers in ecstasy.

From the first, the children gave an example of the proper attitude that we should adopt towards the Blessed Virgin. Spontaneously natural and trusting, they chatted with her, telling her all about the most elementary features of their rural life; they blew her kisses, and she even permitted them to hold her crown in their hands, When the Virgin took her leave, they were saddened. "Don't go yet awhile; you have only been here a second," they often pleaded.

On a certain occasion, one child turned to another. "You know lots of funny stories. Tell her some so she won't go away," she urged.

The spectators were occasionally disappointed by such simple conversations. The same occurred at Lourdes, where Bernadette at first used to answer Our Lady with a seemingly ridiculous "Oui, Mademoiselle."

When the Virgin departed, "vanished into thin air" as the girls described it, they usually bade her farewell with a little wave of the hand.

The visionaries gave the following description of Our Lady: "She

Loli, Conchita and Jacinta in ecstasy.

comes wearing a white robe, a blue mantle and a crown of golden stars; her hands are outstretched with a brown scapular, except when she has the Infant Jesus in her arms. Her dark chestnut hair is long and parted in the middle. Her face is rather long, with a very dainty nose. Her mouth is very pretty, with slightly full lips. She looks about seventeen and is tallish." All four girls stress the unmistakable sound of her voice. "There's no other voice like hers."

She told them that she was Our Lady of Mount Carmel. God willing, once the truth of this story is substantiated, she will come to be venerated under the title of Our Lady of Mount Carmel of Garabandal.

Both the Virgin and the other celestial beings who appeared to the girls were seen full-face. If they moved from one place to another, they usually did so without moving their feet, and facing the visionaries all the time.

The breeze sometimes stirred the Blessed Virgin's hair, which fell in a cascade almost to her waist.

When the Vision disappeared, "we were very sad", says Conchita.

51

The "Summons"

25.—The children exuded joy and happiness after seeing their Heavenly Mother. When they rose early next morning, the first idea that entered their four heads was to return to the scene of the apparition to give thanks for the favor granted them that memorable day. Afterwards, they wended their way home, prepared to obey their respective parents in every way. From that day onwards, they set out to practice Our Lady's instructions as to their conduct in this world.

At school, the teacher. Doña Serafina Gómez, received them with tears in her eyes, smothering them in kisses. She did not tire of exclaiming how lucky they were to have been chosen by God for so exceptional a favor.

As the customary hour of the apparitions approached, the children showed signs of impatience and excitement.

"It's time," their parents pointed out. "Why don't you run along and pray in the lane?"

"She hasn't called us yet," answered the children.

It was the first time that the little girls mentioned what they describe as the *"llamada"* or summons. This is an inner voice which they perceive quite distinctly; a kind of wordless warning that does not come through the ears, but is quite unmistakably heard. A considerable time elapses between the first summons and the second, while the third follows close on the heels of its predecessor.

An investigator of events at Garabandal noted down Jacinta's impressions.

"When the Virgin calls you, does she say 'Jacinta'?"

"The first time," she explained, "she just says 'Jacinta'; the second, 'Jacinta, come'; and the third time, 'Jacinta, hurry, hurry, hurry . . .' But all this is inside me and without actual words

Conchita has received one call, but it is late and she has fallen asleep waiting for the next call.

52

Attempting to give a more graphic description, one child said that, with the summonses, they noticed a refreshing sensation of sorts: "Something like eating a peppermint, but different."

"The inward voice makes you feel very happy," said another. "And, when the third summons comes, you get very fidgety."

Hearing about the summonses, the parish priest arranged to have the little girls separated, leaving Mary Loli and Jacinta at Mary Loli's house, while Mary Cruz and Conchita remained at the latter's. The children indicated when they felt the first call and, later, the second. The instant they received the third summons, the two at Mary Loli's home and the other pair at Conchita's all dashed out at the same time and reached the lane together. There, the Blessed Virgin was waiting for them, bearing the Infant Jesus in her arms.

This time, the Vision had come without the angels. The Virgin and the Infant Jesus were smiling. When asked where St. Michael was, Our Lady's smile broadened.

The Infant Jesus was very little. He looked barely a year old. He did not utter a word, but He was laughing. On occasions, the Virgin allowed the children to hold Him. Then, the spectators observed how they held Him, adopting all the natural postures for cradling a baby. The children said afterwards that He was weightless, but that their hands met an obstruction when they touched Him.

"Come with me," said Mary Cruz to the Infant Jesus, "and I'll give you some candies."

"He didn't say anything, but she talked to us a lot," Conchita commented.

The apparition commenced at half-past seven and ended at eight o'clock.

"God shall be with you, and so shall I," said the Vision. "You will see me again tomorrow."

Owing to the frequency of the visions from then onwards, it is not easy to establish a definite chronological order, or to detail the main features of each occasion. Therefore, except in the case of particular visions where the dialogue was recorded, either on a tape recorder or in shorthand, we shall be obliged only to mention the outstanding points as reported by several eyewitnesses, but without stating exactly in which vision they occurred.

Early in July, people noticed the children picking up little pebbles from the ground and raising them on high for the Vision to kiss. At the moment of offering these stones to be kissed, they dedicated them to particular people. "This one for Andrew . . . This one for Millie . . ." and so on.

It was not long before the pebbles were replaced by pious objects such as rosaries, medals, etc. Wedding rings were very frequently

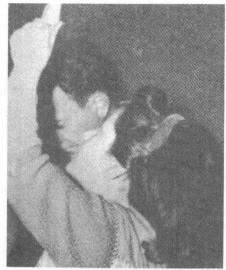

Loli in ecstasy offering the Vision a holy picture to be kissed. Behind her is her father.

offered to be kissed, too. This explains the photographs where the children are seen with thick ropes of rosaries round their necks and their fingers covered in wedding rings.

Curiously enough, if an object was offered to be kissed a second time, when the little visionaries held it up to the Vision, they exclaimed: "Oh, has this one already been kissed?" And on returning it to its owner, they often declared; "The Virgin says this one's already been done."

In their trances, the children's faces underwent a complete change, turning radiant and softly beautiful. This can be observed in the photographs.

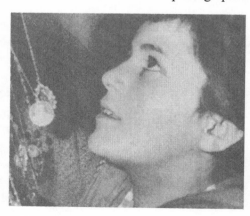

Loli in ecstasy gives the Vision some rosaries to be kissed.

Conchita in ecstasy

The Frequency and Duration of the Visions

26.—Although the visions were not continual for the first two weeks, thenceforth they became more and more frequent. There were often several in a single day. The hour at which the apparitions took place also varied greatly; they occurred early in the morning, at noon, after lunch, etc. The commonest time was from seven to nine in the evening. Later on, they occurred at night, ending as late as five o'clock in the morning on a number of occasions.

Their duration was equally variable. They lasted from two to five minutes in the case of an instantaneous communication, for example: "The Virgin will not be coming today, because there is a group of people who are dancing." Or, "I shall see you again at such-and-such an hour." As a rule, however, the rapture lasted about half an hour, and often enough continued for as long as two hours. Once, Mary Loli remained in ecstasy from 9 p.m. to 5 a.m., with one or two brief intervals.

This is not new in the history of the mystics. St. Teresa writes: "Although it sometimes lasts a long while, on occasions it suddenly ceases, as if the Lord wishes to show that it is not a thing that can be procured by any human means."[†]

[†] St. Teresa of Avila, "Moradas; sextas 2-4".

During the apparitions, time stands still for the visionary. This explains why the girls pleaded: "Oh, but you have only been here a second." They were surprised to hear from the Vision how long the apparition had in fact been in progress. The duration was always confirmed subsequently by the onlookers, a fact that further substantiated the reality of the visions.

It is significant that, in spite of the long periods spent kneeling on the jagged stones in the lane, their heads craned back at an incredible angle, the visionaries never showed signs of the slightest weariness. In summer they were oblivious to the heat and never perspired, despite the breakneck speed of their ecstatic walks. After a rapture, the girls proved to be in a perfectly normal state, relaxed and rested.

The first few visions were of the angel. The same was the case at Fatima. Although some of the visionaries at Garabandal had heard of the apparitions at Fatima, it transpired that none of them knew that these had been heralded by the presence of an angel.

The little girls were restless while waiting for the Virgin, but without experiencing any sensation of fear or uneasiness. It was only at the very beginning, when the shining light prevented them seeing the path, that they felt afraid. But this was immediately followed by an overwhelming peace and joy. To quote the eminent theologian Fr. Royo Marin: "The visions sent by God usually produce great fear at first; but later they leave the soul full of love, humility, tenderness and peace." [†]

Conchita gives her crucifix to be kissed.

27.—The approximate sequence of the apparitions was as follows: from June 18th to July 1st, the children saw the angel, but only on July 1st did he speak to them. On July 2nd, the Blessed Virgin appeared. During the second half of July, they began to experience ecstatic oscillations, swaying to and fro. About August 2nd or 3rd, the first ecstatic falls occurred. And, on August 5th, there commenced the phenomenon of the ecstatic walks of one kind or another, as we shall see.

[†] Fr. Royo Marin, "Teología de la Perfección Cristiana." Section No. 591.

Chapter Four

DETAILS OF A FEW TRANCES

Conchita at the Pines a few moments before receiving
Holy Communion from the Angel

28.—On July 27th, there took place an apparition that has been described in detail by an eyewitness.

In the morning, the children had a vision, announcing another one for eight o'clock that evening.

"It's earlier today," the little girls declared.

At the appointed time, an estimated six hundred people were in San Sebastian de Garabandal awaiting events. There were seven priests and a Dominican professor from the Workers' University of Cordoba.

It was nearly eight o'clock when the four reached the lane. Before they could reach the enclosure, they fell to their knees, two in front and two behind, about eighteen inches apart. Conchita had her head craned back in a very awkward posture nearly all the time. The other three looked ahead, their eyes raised on high. Mary Cruz wept. There was a sweet expression on the four little faces. They occasionally smiled and, once or twice, burst out laughing.

At one juncture, they all held up the masses of medals slung round their necks for the Vision to kiss.

"This one belongs to a man who told me you were to kiss it very hard for him."

Jacinta started one of those swaying motions that were later to end in ecstatic falls. Still in a trance, Mary Cruz put out her arm to prevent Jacinta losing her balance. There came a moment when Jacinta was half-lying on the ground.

"Cross my arms," Conchita requested Mary Loli. "No, you've crossed them the wrong way."

Only a visionary who was not in a state of ecstasy could take hold of another, in a trance, and move her limbs like a doll's to set them in a certain position. Anyone else encountered a rigidity that was difficult to overcome. They could lift one another up with the greatest of ease. On the other hand, two grown men were barely able to move a single child when in a rapture. In one of the photographs, Conchita can be seen, before the church door, lifting Mary Loli up to give something to the Virgin to be kissed. This is a result of the lack of gravity characteristic of the visionaries, and only they can do this to one another.

Photograph taken inside the church. Loli easily lifts Jacinta to help her reach up to the Vision, whereas two grown men can hardly move her.

Conchita in ecstasy, rising after an ecstatic fall;
only half her body is resting on the ground

The cases of levitation that have occurred at Garabandal fall within this same group of phenomena.

In the course of this particular vision—according to the eyewitness report mentioned—Mary Cruz spent the whole time kneeling on a sharp wedge of stone some two inches thick, without any sign of pain or discomfort.

When the time came to say goodbye, they blew kisses into the air and opened and shut their hands in that expressive little wave of farewell so common in small children.

But, first, they pleaded with the Vision not to leave so soon. "An hour already . . . ? Noooo! Only a second . . . An hour an a quarter . . . ? Noooo! Just a short while . . . But it must be, if you say so, 'cause you don't tell fibs."

Conchita repeated the Virgin's words. "An hour and twenty-five minutes." Exactly the time the vision had lasted.

Their return to normality was sudden and of one accord, like electric bulbs when the current is switched off. All four lowered their gaze at the same moment. They recovered their customary speaking voices and said, "let's say the rosary."

I say they recovered their normal voices, because the conversations with Our Lady were carried on in a rather husky whisper. There are several copies of recording tapes with some of these conversations.

In the conversation of that particular day, they asked Our Lady why she had not brought the Infant Jesus with her; they talked to her about some priests who had come; they told her that the parish priest had given them some plums in the sacristy, and that the pulpit was almost falling apart; they said Fr. Marichalar had scolded Conchita for wearing her long mane of hair loose, "like St. Michael's"; and that Conchita's mother was swarthy and only had two teeth . . .

They also mentioned that a film had been taken of them, and that they themselves had never been to the cinema, although they had passed by one in Torrelavega, "and it was a house . . ."

When they spoke of the priests (always a favorite topic in the children's conversations with the Blessed Virgin), they remarked that one of them was wearing a white habit and "shoes with holes in the top", as they described his sandals. They could not recall his Order; it was too much for them. The Vision told them that he was a Dominican. "Yes, the 'Dominicu'." They were very pleased with themselves at having managed to remember it.

Conchita in Santander

29.—Fearing that Conchita, who seemed the brightest of the four, might be influencing the others, some priests and doctors agreed to have her separated from them. She was taken to stay in Santander. There, a close watch was kept on her. She was also taken to see the Apostolic Administrator.

One day, while they were in a state of ecstasy, Mary Cruz, Mary Loli and Jacinta were informed by the Virgin that, at that very moment, Conchita was in a trance, too. "How lovely! She must be seeing you in Santander," the three exclaimed.

Conchita's ecstasy took place in the street, in front of the church of La Consolacion. She went into a trance at the same time as her friends at Garabandal were speaking to the Virgin.

In her diary, Conchita writes that "the police had to give a hand, because there were lots of people all around . . . When the vision ended, they left me in an office with a priest and a doctor. The priest's name was Don Francisco de Odriozola, and the doctor was Dr. Piñal. They said, how had I done these things; and that I was mad, deceiving people in that way. They also said: 'sit up straight and look at my nose. I am going to hypnotize you.' I laughed, and he said to me: 'Don't laugh; it is not a laughing matter!' And that day they didn't do anything more to me."[†]

After calling in several doctors to see her, they decided that she should stay

---

[†] Quoted from Conchita's diary.

on in Santander "to enjoy herself". Accompanied by some little girls her own age, they started to apply the new therapy to cure her. This consisted of taking her to the beach and to funfairs. These two forms of entertainment were novel to her. But her heart was in the mountains, with her playmates and fellow visionaries; and with Our Lady, who was always in her thoughts. "As I was taken to the beach every day, the Virgin didn't appear to me."

After a week of this, a friend of her family's intervened and arranged for her to return home. Her mother went to pick her up. "The doctor got very angry and said lots of things to me so that I shouldn't go home. And I told him that I hadn't seen the Virgin, but that I was sure the others had." And she closes the episode in her diary saying: "They were all very good to me really."

When she arrived back at Garabandal, she encountered "several Padres and a lot of people who were on their way to meet me." Mary Loli and Jacinta, who were in a trance in the church, had just announced "that I was coming up the road, as in fact I was." The Virgin had told them. The people had immediately set out to see if it was true, and had met her on her way up from Cosio. At home once more, Conchita told her friends that, while in Santander, she had only had one vision, but that she had spoken to the Virgin once, without seeing her. "She told me that she did not appear to me more because I went to the beach."

Secret Revelations

30.—On July 29th, the little girls had an ecstasy under the close scrutiny of a doctor, who took their pulse and diagnosed their normality. The spectators were all crowding round, causing a lot of noise and making it difficult to hear the visionaries' words, spoken as they were in that husky whisper. The general din was only increased by the collapse of a rough stone wall onto which a number of onlookers had clambered.

A couple of Civil Guards attempted to restore silence. All at once, the trance concluded. They returned to normality.

"The Virgin says that we're to go up to the pines; and that our parents, the priests, the nuns and the Civil Guards can come, too. But they must remain at a distance. And the rest must stay farther away still."

They climbed the hill to the pine-grove. Calmly, the little girls pointed out the positions that everyone should take up. The Civil Guards made as if to keep the crowd back, but, incredible though it may seem, they obeyed the little visionaries' instructions to the letter.

The Vision had told them that the onlookers might watch, but not hear. She also indicated that the children should be accompanied by two little girls as witnesses. Their names were Mary Carmen and Sari, about six years old at the time.

It was not the first time that these child witnesses had been used. They had also accompanied the visionaries on a few other occasions, on the orders of the Vision. At one point, it was suggested that one of them should be replaced by a bigger girl aged about twelve, but the Vision had not consented to this.

It was in the course of those visions that Our Lady completed her message and revealed a secret to them. They were not allowed to make the message known until October 18th, 1961. This time, their faces were sad during the trance. One parent remarked: "They're crying." Their conversation could not be heard, but there came a sound of kisses being blown to the Vision.

After some minutes, the parish priest called to Mary Carmen, one of the child witnesses. She slowly came over. Asked what they were talking about, she shrugged indifferently: "They're asking the Virgin not to tell them sad things." The requirements of the public remaining at a distance and Mary Carmen's short explanation served to confirm that Our Blessed Mother was telling them about the punishment that divine justice has prepared for Mankind if we disregard Our Lady's messages and do not mend our ways.

One of them finally rose to her feet and took the Virgin's crown in her arms. The crowd saw her go through the motions of examining it, and lift it onto her head. The crown was passed from hand to hand among the children. The spectators could see that it fitted some heads better than others.

An eyewitness recorded the scene. "They raised their hands as if proffering something. One folded her arms. There was a sound of kisses. They stretched out their arms, smiling; now, they were listening; they started to cry. After eleven minutes they came to. We ran over to them and observed that one still had wet tear-stains on her cheeks. 'Why are you crying?' we asked. But she did not answer."[†]

"Who did you see?" someone asked Mary Loli.

"We saw Our Lady of Mount Carmel. We held her crown in our hands."

"We were still talking to them," recalls a spectator, "when they had their third vision of the day, and went into a trance again. This time, everything they said was heard quite clearly. The Virgin brought the Infant Jesus. They took His

---

[†] Verbatim testimony from one of the many accounts quoted here only after due verification.

crown. The little girls remarked that it was small. They asked His age. "The Virgin is very pleased because the people obeyed her. She says to say the rosary. She says that if they want they can come and say it here."

They were back to normal. They started the rosary. When they reached the words "The Lord is with Thee", in the fifth Hail Mary of the third decade, they went into a rapture, their voices trailing off on the last word. It was their fourth vision that day, July 29th. This ecstasy lasted about an hour.

"Why have you come?"

"......................"

"If the people hadn't obeyed, wouldn't you have come?"

"............................"

"So that they'll believe?"

"............................"

They proffered something. They blew a kiss.

"Isn't it lovely!"

They were still absorbed, unblinking.

"You're so sweet . . . Tomorrow we'll fast when we come; we won't eat anything at all . . . "

"............................"

"Shall I kiss your scapular?"

This referred to the scapular that often hung from the Virgin's arm, near her wrist.

"Some Carmelite Padres came today ..."

"............................"

"I'm thinking of the 'Dominicu'."

The memory of this Dominican Father seems to have been deeply engraved on their minds, perhaps on account of his white habit, which they saw for the first time on his visit.

"Show us your robe again. It's white with white flowers on it."

"Isn't it lovely!"

"Let me have your crown! How huge it is!"

"A Civil Guard brought a little girl who can't speak or walk. I promised him . . . Cure her!"

"......................"

"Cure something so everyone can see it."

This dialogue is quoted verbatim direct from the notes jotted down in the course of the ecstasy by a totally trustworthy witness. The witness adds the following comment: "Inside me, there were evolving the first inklings of a train of thought with regard to the hypotheses that I was forming. At that very moment, I was thinking that this might quite well be a case of self-suggestion or hypnosis, and I was looking round me to see if there was anyone nearby who might be responsible for the children's conduct. I was struck by the fact that the children should all be on the same mental scene, and that they should sing in unison and make the Sign of the Cross together. At times, it was almost as if they had but one soul between them. Their reactions were identical. As these thoughts were framed in my mind, one of the girls, Maria Dolores (Mary Loli), came to, whereas Jacinta remained in the same position, still in ecstasy. As Maria Dolores came out of her trance, she turned her head slightly towards me and I asked her: "Can't you see the Virgin?"

"No, *Señor*:"

"Why not?"

"She's gone," was the brief reply.

"Look at Jacinta." Mary Loli glanced at Jacinta, who was still in ecstasy. Seeing Jacinta's face and expression, she smiled. It was the first time she had seen one of her fellow visionaries in ecstasy while she herself was normal.

"What did the Virgin say to you?" I asked, after she had watched Jacinta for a few minutes. She was on the point of replying when she was once again rooted to the spot, her head clicking back, oblivious to the world around her. There ensued the following dialogue:

"Ah, Loli's back again . . . ! Where've you been, Loli? Why did you go away?" Jacinta demanded.

"Why did you go away?" Loli asked the Vision. There was a pause, and then they both said: "Oh, so that's why, is it?" And Mary Loli added: "It's so he'll believe."

I immediately thought that the "so he'll believe" must refer to myself, since it fitted in perfectly with my inner thoughts and broke the uniformity in the actions of the two children." [†]

"Ohhh. She's gone . . ." they both exclaimed. Their return to normal lasted a split second.

[†] Quoted from a report by Fr. Ramon Maria Andreu, S.J., verified from other testimony.

Chapter Five

FROM JULY 30th to AUGUST 3rd

Conchita in ecstasy raises towards the Vision the scapular of one of the two Brothers of St. John of God, between whom she is seen standing after the ecstasy.

31.—On the 30th and 31st of July, they also had several visions. On the 30th, they insistently begged for proof so that everyone might believe.

"Let it happen at night, in broad daylight." When they said this, it was dark, and their confusion is hardly surprising, for they themselves were bathed in the light of the Vision,

"The Virgin looks very grave when we ask her for a miracle."

Mary Loli had a vision at her grandmother's. "Why have you come to me here, where nobody can see?" she queried. In their desire to convince people of the reality of their visions, they preferred the rapture to overtake them out-of-doors for everyone to see, and not just for themselves in private.

It was on the 31st that people were amazed to see the visionaries walking along on their knees for the first time. They felt as though the Virgin were receding from them, and they instinctively closed the distance, without getting to their feet.

That day, they also recited the rosary in ecstasy without counting on their fingers. They did not make any mistakes in the number of

Hail Marys, because the Virgin told them when it was time for the "Glory be to the Father". "Sometimes, Our Lady said the Hail Mary with us, but only to teach us to say it right."

On the 31st, Mary Loli experienced the phenomenon of ecstatic oscillations. Jacinta was in front of Mary Loli and so could not see her. But, she had a presentiment that her friend was on the point of over-balancing and, reaching out backwards, without once turning her head, she steadied her on several occasions.

The onlooker's field of vision was different to the visionaries'. In ecstasy, they could only see one another. On coming out of their trance, they lost their reciprocal vision. But a visionary who was in the normal state was placed on an intermediate plane of vision. She could not see the apparition, but she could establish mental or verbal contact with the others who were in a trance. The rest of the spectators were unable to do this.

Besides being able to speak to one another, they found it fairly easy to move the stiff limbs of the visionary in a trance. Others found their members quite rigid, as if paralyzed.

32.—On August 1st, there were three visions; at 10:45 a.m., 12:15 p.m. and 3:40 p.m.

During one of these, the little girls said the Hail Mary with the inclusion of the following expression: ". . . Holy Mary, Mother of God *and our Mother .* . ." The Vision told them that she thought it was very nice, but that they should not use this formula again until it was introduced by the Church.

In all cases, people were struck by the Vision's respect for established liturgy.

In view of the great similarity between the ensuing ecstasies and dialogues, we shall skip the details except when there is some peculiarity worth mentioning.

33.—During the third vision that day, they requested the Blessed Virgin to kiss a pebble which they had ready for a priest who had come from abroad. The visionary attempted to pronounce the name, but could not manage it. "It sounds like Canarias," (Canary Islands), the child said, "but that's not the name . . ." She finally gave up. "You say it!" There was a pause as she listened to the Vision. "That's right, Caracas!"

The name might have been said in a low voice by an onlooker. But the visionary could not have heard it in any case, because she was in that state of anesthesia and total isolation produced by the trance. She was referring to Fr. Cipriano Abad, who had in fact just returned from Caracas.

34.—Let us pass on to the second vision, at five past nine, on August 3rd. It was during this vision that Jacinta and Mary Loli experienced their first ecstatic fall. Afraid lest she had come to any harm, Jacinta's mother threw herself forward to catch her. Mary Loli was caught by a member of the authorities from Madrid who had come to Garabandal.

The two little girls fell to the ground simultaneously, but quite unconscious. In spite of the awkward posture that they were in, they continued to see everything as usual, and to experience those moments of profound bliss in the world of their vision. In the accompanying photographs the children can be seen on the ground and on a kitchen floor. Turned upside down, these photographs show the blissful, smile on Mary Loli's face, despite her awkward posture.

An eyewitness reported that "the postures that they adopt in their falls are generally very beautiful, like sculptures. They cannot be recalled—at least I have not seen them—ever to have adopted postures that were indecorous or indecent. They may remain on the ground for a moment, or they may lie there for several minutes. When they all fall together, both the fall and the movement of getting up are usually synchronized. Generally speaking, they form a beautiful ensemble."

To quote Fr. Royo Marin: "The positions of a person in ecstasy are highly varied, but always dignified and decorous."[†]

On August 3rd, they fell on the altar steps in the church, and remained reclining in that position for about thirty minutes. It was there that they asked the Vision for news of Conchita, and she told the children that their friend was on her way back to Garabandal. A few minutes later, they repeated their question.

"Ah! she's back home," they were heard to say. And so it turned out. Conchita had just that moment arrived from Santander.

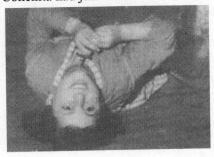

Ecstatic fall: Loli

[†] Fr. Royo Marn, "Teología de la Perfección Cristiana", Section No. 463.

35.—At first, people did not take part in the apparitions, and the little girls were alone in their world. It was not long, however, before the public began to join in, saying the rosary aloud and asking for objects to be kissed by the Vision. From that time onwards, the children mentioned people by name in their dialogues. They even located several people and touched them. In such cases, although they could not see the people in question, they could feel them as long as they were connected with what the visionaries were doing or saying at the time. If the contact was with someone else, the children felt nothing, due to their total insensibility to the outside world.

When they returned a medal or rosary and tried to place it over the owner's head, they commonly said to the Vision: "You take my hands and move them, because I can't see." The movement then became much quicker, and so precise that the visionaries put the rosary or chain in place without even touching the head.[†]

From all that we have seen so far, the reader will have grasped the naturalness and familiarity with which they addressed Our Lady, always using the Spanish familiar form of *"tú"* and absolutely spontaneous expressions. Is this what Our Heavenly Mother wants from us, her children?

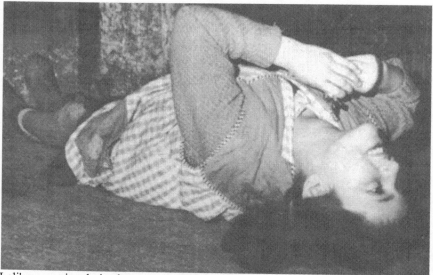

Loli's expression during her ecstatic fall leaves no doubt as to the beauty and reality of her vision.

[†] The visionaries returned objects to their owners in ecstasy, without taking their eyes off the Vision. Hence, they executed their movements without looking at the person in question.

Chapter Six

THE PRODIGIES CONTINUE

L: Conchita used to wear tresses, but had her hair cut short (R.) in Santander.

36.—On August 4th, Mary Loli and Jacinta went into an ecstasy in the pine-grove. The trance followed the customary pattern: they proffered medals and rosaries to be kissed, fell on their backs, etc. Then, they got to their knees again and Jacinta addressed the Virgin.

"Conchita's back. They cut her plaits in Santander. She's very pretty and brown, 'cause she went to the beach."

Coming to, they answered several questions asked by those around them. One bystander had a tape recorder and he showed it to the children.

"If you see the Virgin again, tell her to speak into it."

They were in the midst of this conversation, when they went into a rapture once more. Mary Loli, who had entered her trance before she had time to relinquish the microphone, held it up.

"Go on; you speak, so people will believe . . ." she coaxed the Vision. "Why not? Go on. Say something, do . . ."

At the end of the trance, they listened to the conversation recorded on the tape. Reaching the point in question, they distinctly heard a very sweet voice say softly over the loud-speaker: "No, I shall not speak"

Everyone was completely taken aback. The owner of the tape recorder jumped up, crying: "I'm sending this to the Pope." They rewound the tape and played it back, but the voice had disappeared. Crestfallen, they made their way down the hill to Mary Cruz's house. There, they switched on the tape recorder once more. This time, everyone heard the mysterious voice. The visionaries assured them that it was the Virgin's voice. The tape was rewound, and they listened again and again, but the only thing to be heard was the monologue of the little visionaries.

Can their ears have been playing tricks on them? Was it self-suggestion? That we shall never know. We can only go by the evidence of those who were present at the time. Accounts of this strange occurrence have been given by several different witnesses, each in his own fashion, but they all coincide in the essentials. These accounts are in writing, and signed by the following witnesses: Don Gaudencio Cepeda Palacios, aged 33, from Torquemada; Don Jeronimo Diez Serrano, 38, from Cabezón de Liébana; Don Agustín Pinay Martmez, 40, from Santillana del Mar; Don Luis Toribio Millán, 38, from Aguilar del Campo; Don José Salceda Calderón, 42, likewise from Aguilar del Campo; Dona Maria del Rosario and Doña María Elisa Salceda, the latter's daughters.

A striking picture of Loli and Jacinta walking in ecstasy. Behind Loli is her father Ceferino.

70

Ecstatic Walks

37.—That August 4th also saw the first walk in ecstasy. In their ecstasy, the children walked either forwards or backwards. In fact, they did not need their eyes to see the way, for they were guided by the inner light of the visions.

On the 5th, they descended from the pines to the church in an ecstatic walk at breakneck speed. It was almost impossible to stop them, for they acquired tremendous impetus in their forward movements. Conchita was heard to ask forgiveness for having been to the beach, and she insisted on the need for a miracle so that everyone might believe.

During a nocturnal ecstasy on the 6th, they recited the rosary. At twelve minutes past ten, they came out of the trance, which had begun at half past nine. Fully conscious, they proceeded to say a decade to the Blessed Sacrament. The people present were overwhelmed by the contrast between the voice, speed and devotion of the children's prayers in ecstasy and in a normal state. "When in a trance, their concentration and devotion is breath-taking," said one witness.

On August 7th, they had their first vision at 2 p.m. Our Lady told them to stay at home and not go out. These instructions were part of the wonderful protection that the Virgin afforded them, thanks to which they never had a mishap, despite the masses of people from every walk of life who were flocking to Garabandal at that period. As a rule, the order to stay indoors came on days when the largest crowds gathered.

Loli and Jacinta walk in ecstasy, without taking their eyes off the Apparition, smiling all the while, or crying with the Vision.

71

That day, Mary Loli lost a rosary. Unable to find it, she asked the Vision its whereabouts. The Virgin told her the exact spot where she would discover it. It was not the only time this happened. On several occasions, what with ecstatic falls and walks, medals and other pious objects were lost amidst the piles of other objects given to the children. They were retrieved by asking the Virgin for a detailed description of their whereabouts.

The ecstatic walks took different forms. At times, the four girls moved forwards together at normal speed. On other occasions, they started together only to separate later, each taking a different street and then joyously meeting up at another spot. They frequently advanced at such a speed that it became very difficult to keep up with them. At times, they advanced on their knees and, once, even sitting down. To quote the authority, Fr. Royo Marin: "There have been saints who, during their ecstasy, used to speak with the object of their contemplative Vision and even advance in an ecstatic walk. In this respect, the cases of St. Catherine of Siena and St. Magdalena de Paccis are well-known examples.[†]

The children are here seen walking backwards in ecstasy; their eyes remain fixed on their vision.

[†] Fr. Royo Marin, "Teología de la Perfección Cristiana," Section No. 467.

Fr. Luis' Visit

Rev. Luis Andrew, S.J.

38.—August 8th, 1961, is one of the most memorable dates in the story of Garabandal.

Twenty people set out from Aguilar del Campo at six o'clock in the morning, in five cars. Among them was Fr. Luis Maria Andreu of the Society of Jesus.

They reached Garabandal that morning, and the parish priest in Cosio handed over to Fr. Luis the key of the village church, for he himself had to go to Torrelavega that day. Conchita, Jacinta and Mary Loli received Holy Communion and, after Mass, they said that Our Lady had announced a vision for 2 p.m. in the church.

Fr. Luis Andreu always celebrated Mass with great devotion, but that day even more so, as testified by members of the congregation. At first, they put it down to the presence of the visionaries

Fr. Luis celebrating his first Mass.

Afterwards, it was connected with the fact that that was to be Fr. Luis' last Mass, a circumstance which intuition had perhaps told him. Some put it down to a little incident. When he was handed the wine cruet, it was found to be empty. His server was obliged to fetch wine from a house nearby, although afraid that it might not be in a fit condition to celebrate Mass. He communicated this fear to Fr. Luis, who closed his eyes, joined his hands and, after a few moments of prayer, nodded his head in assent and continued the Mass. All this, together with the visions of the eve and the ones expected that same day, may have contributed to the devotion and general fervor at Mass that day. The fact is that, after Mass, the congregation commented on the silence, piety and general devoutness with which they and the celebrant had taken communion before the altar.

At 12:10 p.m., the children went into an ecstasy. Conchita was heard to insist on the need for a public miracle. "At Lourdes and Fatima you gave them proof . . ." She smiled. "D'you want me to show you what I've got?" She held up seven or eight rosaries. "You're to kiss them ..."................... "Someone brought us some dolls, today".................. "How d'you like me with my hair short?".................. "You're coming this afternoon? Oh, how lovely!"

Jacinta proceeded. "Have we got to stay two in each house again this afternoon?".................. "How old are you?".................. "You're three years older than me ...".................. "Six?".................. "Oh, yes, of course. Twelve and six makes eighteen. You're seven years older than Mary Cruz; she's eleven."

They then asked her why the angel had not returned, and commented on the arrival of some priests who had come to Garabandal for the first time. "One of them said Mass very slowly and very nicely."

"When we ask you for proof, why do you look so grave? It's nearly two months now," Conchita queried.

"Give it now, right away," insisted Mary Loli. "You always say you'll give it in time, in time. . ."

They walked backwards as far as the altar of Our Lady of the Rosary. There, they recited the rosary with touching devotion and had a fall in ecstasy. Finally, they were told what time to expect the Vision that evening.

This dialogue is quoted, after due verification, from the notebooks of Don Andres Pardo, Fr. Valentin Marichalar and Fr. Luis Maria Andreu, simply to stress yet again the amazing familiarity and naturalness of the children's conversations with Our Blessed Mother. Many feel that it should serve as an example to us all.

"A Miracle, A Miracle!"

39.—At 9:35 p.m., on August 8th, the second vision of the day commenced. All four children fell in ecstasy at the foot of the steps to the high altar. They heaved a sigh.

"Yes, as you wish, as you command . . . We haven't given any proof yet, and people don't believe.... I don't mind going all over the place. Anything you say...."

They rose to their feet and left the church in ecstasy, prepared to make a tour of all the spots where they had had apparitions.

"When's the next time we'll see you, so the people can come? I heard people saying it's an illness we've got, and the little kids throw stones at us ... If you're pleased with us, then it's all the same to us....."

In no time they had climbed the hillside to the pines. Mary Loli was trembling.

"Yes, this is where the chapel's going to be built . . . This is a good spot. . . Shall we kneel down?" They knelt and sang the hymn to St. Michael. They kissed something in the air. At that moment, Fr. Luis Andreu looked deeply moved. He turned pale and repeated four times, in a distinct voice: "A miracle, a miracle . . ."

The little girls retraced their steps to the church, after what Fr. Luis described as "an impressive descent" from the pines. Conchita realized that she had lost a rosary that had been entrusted to her.

"I've lost the rosary; it was the student's," she said to the Vision. "I'm so upset. Will he scold me? Eh? Where did I drop it? Up the hill. Higher up than where we saw you?"

They said the rosary, led by Mary Loli and Conchita.

These notes are taken from Fr. Luis' note-book. *They were the last lines that he was ever to write.*

In their descent from the pines, "the children seemed to have wings on their heels".[†] They lost two rosaries on the way down. One belonged to Fr. Luis, and was mislaid by Mary Loli, although the Virgin told her where it had fallen. The other belonged to the "student", a seminarian called Don Andres Pardo.

Mary Loli wanted to run and fetch it at once, but it was very late.

"Not now; it's late. Tomorrow, in daylight, you can go and find it, and, *if I don't come back again,* you keep it safe and give it to my brother when he comes, because he'll certainly come," Fr. Luis said.

[†] The words of Fr. Royo Marin.

The child found it without trouble, because the Virgin had told her where it had fallen, and under exactly which stone it was lying.

This fact is significant. The rosary in question was the size of a half dollar, a finger rosary of the type with a large hole so that it can be made to revolve around a finger. It was lost in pitch darkness in the course of a fast run up a stretch of mountainside. The child to whom it had been entrusted told the Vision of its loss and, after a few brief directions, identified the stone under which it lay.

Mary Loli kept the rosary very carefully until Fr. Ramon Andreu came. For, as his brother had assured her before his death, Fr. Ramon was bound to come to get it.

"Today is the happiest day of my life."

40.—What happened in Don Rafael Fontaneda's car, in which Fr. Luis Andreu was travelling, on August 8th and in the early hours of the 9th, is best told by Señor Fontaneda himself. He was driving home from Garabandal accompanied by his wife, their daughter, the chauffeur, Don Jose Salceda and Fr. Luis himself. This is his version, written only a few hours afterwards.

"That day, August 8th, we met Fr. Valentin Marichalar, parish priest of Cosio and San Sebastian de Garabandal, and he handed over to Fr. Luis the keys to the church, requesting him to stand in as parish priest, since he himself had to go to Torrelavega. I noticed that Fr. Luis was looking very pleased. "Faito," he called to me, "I'm parish priest of Garabandal for the day." And he joked about it.

The Mass which he celebrated in the church at San Sebastian was thought by many of the congregation to be very moving indeed.

The children had an ecstasy that morning. Fr. Luis stood close by them and, as on previous occasions, took notes of everything they did and said. During this trance, there were moments when Fr. Luis seemed totally absorbed. At one juncture, those nearest him could see tears on his cheeks; silent tears that appeared to be caused by some special realization that he was witnessing something extraordinary.

When I mentioned this to his brother Fr. Ramon Maria Andreu, the following day, he was very much surprised, for he had never seen his brother betray his emotion in that way. "I've never seen him cry," he said.

That afternoon, the children's ecstasy took them up to the pines and down again at tremendous speed. Throughout the time that they spent in the pine-grove. Fr. Luis examined them very closely. It was as though he did not want to miss a single detail of what

76

was happening. We suddenly noticed what seemed to be a flood of emotion overtake him, and he repeated the words, "A miracle, a miracle!" four times over, in a loud and obviously deeply moved voice. Then, he fell silent, and the children started the descent, remarking in ecstasy that they were going to the church. As usual, they said this in their conversation with the Virgin.

They made the descent to the church at whirlwind speed. Fr. Royo Marin, O.P., told everybody where they were making for. "Run to the church. The children have got wings on their heels."

Some of us walked down from San Sebastian de Garabandal to Cosio, while others descended in a jeep. Out of deference to the cloth, Fr. Luis was made to go in the jeep. I saw that he looked very happy. My relatives who drove with him tell me that he expressed his happiness in no uncertain terms, and also spoke of his absolute certainty as to the truth of the visionaries' claims.

Once in Cosio, those of us on the expedition got into our vehicles and, although asked to drive home in my sister's car, Fr. Luis chose to join me, since he had come with me in the first place.

On the back seat of the car sat my wife Carmen, my daughter Mary Carmen, aged eight, and myself. Those in front were Jose Salceda, who was at the wheel, and Fr. Luis.

Almost the whole way, we spoke of all we had seen that day. Fr. Luis told me that he had discussed matters with Fr. Royo Marin, and that they had agreed on every point. Both my wife and I, and Jose Salceda, too, noticed an air of immense happiness in Fr. Luis, as well as absolute certainty in what he said. He spoke unhurriedly, and repeated over and over: "How happy I am!", "I'm full of joy! What a present the Virgin has given me! There can't be the slightest doubt any longer that what is happening to the children is true." We proceeded to chat in this vein for a time. At Puentenansa, we stopped to quench our thirst. Fr. Luis had an unchilled soft-drink.

At Torrelavega, we came across a jeep that had made the trip with some other people from Aguilar del Campo. It was the same vehicle that had driven us up the trail to San Sebastian de Garabandal. We halted to see if they were in trouble. José Salceda and Fr. Luis got out and talked with them for a while.

On the second stage of the drive home, I asked: "Father, why don't you sleep for a while?" He assented and slept for about an hour, until shortly before we reached Reinosa. On awaking, he said: "I must have slept very soundly. I feel completely rested. I am not at all tired."

We were all feeling sleepy, for it was four o'clock in the morning. Near Reinosa, we stopped to drink at a public water fountain. We resumed our journey. After entering the town, Fr. Luis repeated once again the words that had never been far from his lips all during that drive through the night. "I feel overwhelmed with joy. What a wonderful present the Virgin has given me! How lucky to have a Mother like that in Heaven! We shouldn't be afraid of the supernatural. The children have given us an example of the attitude we should take to the Blessed Virgin. I haven't the slightest doubt that this business of the children is true. Why can she have chosen us? Today is the happiest day of my life."

Having said this, he fell silent. I asked him a question. Not obtaining an answer, I asked him: "Father, is something wrong?" I thought he must be feeling car-sick. "No, nothing; sleepy," came the reply. His head bowed forward onto his chest, and he made a slight coughing sound.

José Salceda turned towards Fr. Luis. Observing that his eyes had turned upwards, he said: "The Padre has been taken very bad." My wife grasped his wrist and, feeling no pulse, cried out: "Stop, his pulse has stopped; there's a hospital here." Believing him to be car-sick, I had tried to open the door as soon as the car pulled to a stop. "Don't worry, Father; it's nothing serious. You'll get over it in a minute," I reassured him. My wife said: "Let's take him to the hospital." "Don't talk nonsense," I replied. But, she insisted. "Yes, he's unconscious."

We had stopped some five or ten yards beyond the hospital door. We rang the bell, and a nurse opened the door immediately. Seeing Fr. Luis, she at once declared that he was dead. She nevertheless gave him an injection.

Meanwhile, José Salceda went in search of a priest and a doctor. The doctor was on the spot within ten minutes. His name was Dr. Vicente Gonzalez. He could do no more than confirm that Fr. Luis was dead. An instant later, the parish priest arrived and administered the last Sacraments.

After the first few minutes of bewilderment and nervousness, I telephoned Fr. Ramon Andreu, who was giving a retreat at a convent in Valladolid.

A few hours later, Fr. Royo Marin arrived to keep us company and console us. My brother and sister and brother-in-law drove over from Aguilar del Campo, and Fr. Ramon Andreu arrived about mid-morning.

Whenever my wife and I have recalled those scenes, which made such a deep impression on us, we have felt a sensation of peace and unmistakable serenity. The first thing that occurred to us to say, and the many occasions when we were asked our opinion of Fr. Luis' death, was this: "He died of joy."

In spite of the fact that it only took a split second for him to pass from absolute normality to death, Fr. Luis died with a smile on his lips.

I asked his brother, Fr. Ramon, what precedents there were in the family for heart trouble, and he told me there were none. Fr. Luis' only ailment was hay fever in spring, but it did not prevent him carrying on with his ordinary duties. His doctors had prescribed some pills to offset this hay fever.

On August 8th, he descended to Cosio by jeep. He cannot, therefore, have been more tired than any of the rest of us. On top of having been on our feet all day in San Sebastian de Garabandal, we had afterwards trudged four and a half miles down the mountain spur to Cosio on foot.

The previous year, when he was Professor of Theology at Oña, he frequently played *"pelota"* or *"jai-alai"* on the courts there, and used to go walking through the countryside, on holidays, in the company of other professors. Indeed, he referred to these leisure hours on several occasions while staying with us.

Shortly afterwards, at San Sebastian de Garabandal, the children informed me that the Virgin had told them that Fr. Luis had seen her when he cried out "A miracle, a miracle!" while in the pine-grove. Later, when I was present during the conversations that they held with Fr. Luis' voice, all those sad scenes of the dawn of August 9th, 1961, acquired a special significance for me, with God's Providence and the love of the Virgin Mary playing an all-important part in it.

"This is the happiest day of my life," Fr. Luis had said. I wanted to ask him what he meant by that, because the happiest day in a priest's life should be the day of his ordination. But he did not give me time. He forestalled me with an answer that ushered him into eternal happiness.

Fr. Royo Marin said to us: "Really and truly, the day one reaches God's arms is the happiest day of one's life."

This is what happened at 4:20 a.m., on August 9th, 1961, on our way home from San Sebastian de Garabandal.

Just to show how gentle this transition from life to death was, let me add that my eight-year old daughter, who was travelling in the car with us, went to bed when we got home to Aguilar del Campo, and slept alone all night long without being the slightest bit afraid or uneasy.

I had with me a crucifix which had previously been kissed by the Vision at Garabandal, and this I put to Fr. Luis' lips and later gave to Fr. Ramon Andreu, who treasures it."

41.—But this is not the end of the story of Fr. Luis. The most surprising part of all took place a few days later, when the children declared that they had spoken to him. They stated that they had seen a light, like those that accompanied the Visions, and that from this light had come the voice of Fr. Luis. On some occasions, these conversations took place in the presence of his brother, Fr. Ramon Andreu. When he heard the children say that they had spoken to his brother, he at first dismissed the entire series of phenomena as a fabrication on the part of the excessively impressionable little girls. He believed that having been upset by his brother's death, they had now taken to saying that they could speak to him just as they had formerly done with the Virgin, which was doubtless the fruit of their imaginations, too. Much to his surprise, however, he heard the children holding a conversation in ecstasy, and realized that they were discussing matters that were known only to the two brothers. They proceeded to speak of some details of the last few days, and of his death. Some of these details were unknown, even to Fr. Ramon, and it was only afterwards that they were verified. During their talk, the children even heard words in foreign languages which they had difficulty in pronouncing.

As a result of this extraordinary series of events, Fr. Andreu's mother entered a Salesian convent and took her vows on April 19th, 1962, thus realizing an ambition that she had discussed with her son Luis about ten years before his death.

The author with Fr. Luis' brothers, three of whom are Jesuits (Marcelino, Ramón and Alejandro).

Chapter Seven

ODDS AND ENDS

42.—If what the children claim is true, the Virgin Mary virtually "lived" in San Sebastian de Garabandal for two whole years. Hence, the difficulty in giving detailed accounts of her constant apparitions. The visionaries were in ecstatic trances at all hours of the day and night. She appeared to them morning, noon and night. The village was constantly crammed with strangers who spent their whole time contemplating these mystical phenomena, hardly pausing to take time out to sleep or eat.

The better to convey the nature of these happenings, in this chapter we shall outline the main features of a series of trances, only quoting totally trustworthy witnesses, and recounting a few anecdotes and peculiarities, to enable the reader to get a true perspective of events at Garabandal by adding these details to the other general information.

Concern for Priests

43.—"She wishes priests to come, above all," the children said over and over again after one of their visions, on August 14th, 1961. They continually insisted on this, later showing a particular interest in priests, both in their prayers and in the reception that they gave all members of the clergy who came to visit them.

That same night, Conchita, Jacinta and Mary Loli walked in ecstasy. Without any prior agreement, they wended their way to Mary Cruz's door, where all three sang in unison:

"Levántate, Mary Cruz,
que viene la Virgen buena
con un cestillo de flares
para su niña pequeña." [†]

They went on to sing some more verses in the same vein. This phenomenon of their breaking out into little improvised songs with unquestionably catchy tunes occurred on several occasions. It is all a part of the artistic gifts found in mystics when in a trance. In his work *"Teologia de*

[†] "Get up, Mary Cruz, get up,
For the good Virgin Mary has come With a little basket of flowers
For you her little one."

la Perfeccion Cristiana" Fr. Royo Marin says in connection with this: "We are going to group together a series of mystical phenomena which, although not visions, locutions or revelations, as such, are connected in a way with the mind, too. These are certain special talents for the arts and science that some people receive through divine inspiration ..."

The Voice of Fr. Luis

44.—On the 16th, they spoke to Fr. Luis. They asked him what he had seen when he cried out "a miracle" several times over. He gave them certain message's for his brother. The little girls reported that they had not seen him, but had heard him speak in exactly the same voice he had used while alive. His voice proceeded "from a light like the sun, with rays falling from it."

On the evening of the 20th, the children continued an interrupted conversation held with Fr. Luis before his death; they asked him to teach them words in foreign languages. Witnesses noted down the words that the visionaries repeated after him, first in French, then in Latin, and finally in German.

The importance of this does not lie so much in the words themselves, but in the way the children repeatedly corrected themselves when their pronunciation was wrong, until they got it right. They gave the impression of truly repeating the words after their teacher.

Then, one of the girls asked several questions, from which could be gleaned a description of Fr. Luis Andreu's winding-sheet and astounding details of his funeral. These were not even known to his brother, who was present during the conversations and could not get over his amazement. The details were all fully confirmed later.

During another trance, Fr. Luis taught them the "Hail Mary" in Greek.

When they next witnessed an apparition and asked where Fr. Luis was, the Blessed Virgin simply smiled. "After all, what need is there for you to tell us, when we already know," the children commented.

Mary-Cruz and Loli in ecstasy (1962)

Neither sleepy nor tired

45.—When the children waited up all night in the hopes of a vision, but finally did not have one, they needed to make up for their lost sleep. On the other hand, if they went into a trance, they seemed not to require the sleep lost during the vision. So it was that Loli sometimes went to bed at six o'clock in the morning and rose for Mass at nine, without showing the slightest signs of weariness later in the day.[†]

On coming out of a trance on August 21st, Jacinta declared that "The Virgin went away because there's a group of people drinking and singing". This fact was verified; several people were discovered making fun of the events at the village and showing signs of being the worse for drink.

The children were never worried and always certain of what they saw. They never argued or attempted to convince anyone, because they declared that the Blessed Virgin had told them repeatedly that "those who do not believe will believe in the end."

When the Bishop ordered the church to be locked to prevent any possible irreverence, the children told the Vision. She recommended them to obey their parents, and especially priests, at all times.

When they made the Sign of the Cross, the little girls imitated the Vision, their actions full of an unmistakable dignity that they could hardly have acquired without having a model before them to copy.

In a trance at half-past three on August 1st, Jacinta turned to Mary Loli, who was showing the Vision a sheet of paper on which she had written the words of the hymn to St. Michael. "But, if you hold the writing towards yourself, how do you expect her to read it?" laughed Jacinta.

On July 31st, Mary Cruz, Jacinta and Mary Loli were in a trance when, all of a sudden, Mary Cruz and Jacinta came to. Their transition from ecstasy to normality was gentle as usual. Seeing Mary Loli still in an ecstasy, and observing the direction of her gaze, Mary Cruz frowned in puzzlement. "What's she looking over there for? She should be looking a little more in this direction."

Mary Cruz had not had a vision for several days when the Virgin appeared with the Infant Jesus for her benefit alone. She told Mary Cruz all about her recent talks with the others. Mary Cruz undoubtedly missed some of these visions because her family had forbidden her to leave the house.

[†] A phenomenon reminiscent of Theresa Neumann. See page 71 onwards in "Estigmatizados y Apariciones".

83

Spirit of Obedience

46.—At one o'clock in the morning of August 25th, Conchita was at home waiting for her third summons, for she had already received two. Fr. Marichalar had devised a ruse with the parish priest from Rivadesella and another priest.

"I'm going to give you three warnings. If the Virgin doesn't call you before the last one, you'll go up to bed," he said to her.

Fr. Marichalar left and returned shortly afterwards. "In a few moments I'll be back to send you to bed."

No sooner had he uttered these words than the child went into ecstasy.

On August 29th, in view of the large crowds, Conchita's brother asked the parish priest whether he thought he should carry the visionary indoors. Fr. Marichalar shrugged his shoulders. After a tremendous struggle, due to the increased weight of the visionaries while in a trance, the youth eventually succeeded in carrying her into the house, leaving the door open. But Conchita at once rose to her feet and walked out. She said that the Virgin had instructed her to tell her brother not to pick her up again when she was in a trance.

That same day, she touched the scapular that the Vision usually wore hanging from her wrist. "It wasn't made of cloth, or of paper, or of wood, or of metal, or of flesh; she couldn't say what it was made of . . ." reports one of her questioners.

On August 30th, while in a rapture, she was heard to remark: "How shameful if Don Valentin finds out. If he's present and hears, he'll jot it all down on his little note-pad."

In their conversations of the 31st, at the parish priest's behest, the children asked the Virgin whether she was there in body and soul. Mary Loli answered on the Virgin's behalf that she was not there in body and soul, but under another form, but that it was she. She said that the Blessed Virgin's parents were called Joachim and Anne, and her husband was St. Joseph. She also said that priests might go to the village, but that if the Bishop had forbidden this, then the first thing was to obey. They also inquired whether she minded their asking her questions. She replied that they might ask about matters connected with the Church, but not silly questions such as they had sometimes put.

The village church is usually locked at nightfall, but the door is left ajar in the daytime. On September 5th, the visionaries walked into the church in ecstasy. Fr. Marichalar soon appeared and ushered the onlookers outside. The only people left in the church were the visionaries and their parents.

"On orders from His Excellency the Bishop, you are to leave," he said. The children instantly emerged from their trance and walked out into the open air. Asked by the parish priest why they had entered, the unanimous reply was that "the Virgin had told them to."

Devotion to the Blessed Sacrament

47.—In their conversations stress was laid on the special veneration due among the saints to St. Joseph as Mary's spouse. The visionaries were also recommended to pray before the Blessed Sacrament since the Blessed Sacrament is "the best thing there is in churches," as the children put it.

On September 8th, the parish priest told them to inquire of the Vision the reason why the phenomena took place at night. A shadow of sadness fell across the Virgin Mary's countenance at this question.

It seems that the Blessed Virgin chose the hours when most offense was given to Our Lord. Perhaps the late hour was also intended to test the spirit of penitence of all who went to Garabandal.

Indeed, in this way the public was selected, for the discomfort of a vigil under the circumstances prevalent at Garabandal requires self-sacrifice. This "selection" of the public in the Marian apparitions has always been achieved by the lateness of the hour, the distance to be covered or the weather. On the day of the miracle of the sun at Fatima, pilgrims who reached the spot had to plod along muddy trails all the previous night. Until recently, it was extremely difficult to drive up to Garabandal by car, and on the day chosen to make the Message known, it poured with rain, as we shall see.

In one trance, the three children went home to change their dresses for longer ones, at the Vision's command. "We should always wear our dresses this long, and especially when we come to see you," said Conchita to the Vision.

In most of their trances, it became the custom for the children to offer objects to the Vision to be kissed. These had to be pious objects. Decorative rings were rejected, the only ones accepted being wedding-rings. Many a time, there was the "miracle" of their being returned. Sightless, the visionaries groped for the owner of the ring in question and unerringly placed it on the correct finger. In one such ecstasy, Mary Loli started to place a wedding-ring on the owner's right hand, as is customary in most parts of Spain. All at once, still gazing upwards, she said: "Oh, not on this one." Withdrawing the ring, she fitted it on the corresponding finger of the left hand. The woman in question was from Valencia, a province where wedding-rings are customarily worn on the left hand, not the right.

Only on one occasion did the Vision admit an object that everyone expected to be rejected, a powder-compact. The child said to the Virgin: "Ah. So it has held the Body of Jesus, has it?" It transpired that this powder-compact had been used during the Spanish Civil War to carry Holy Communion to the sick.

In an apparition on September 15th, the Vision told them not to use cosmetics. One of the children had varnished her finger-nails for fun, and the others had rouged their lips, although they had removed the cosmetics at once. They explained that "the Virgin had seen them doing it at Ceferino's."

On September 17th, Conchita slipped a rather small ring on. When she attempted to remove it, she found that it was stuck fast. Even soap and water would not do the trick. She later went into a trance and, when the moment came to give the wedding-rings to the apparition to kiss, the ring that had obstinately refused to budge slid smoothly off.

On September 19th, Mary Loli, who was in ecstasy, was asked how many priests were in the village at that moment. She answered that there were three, and one "dressed as a Civil Guard". It turned out that an Army chaplain was in Garabandal.

On September 21st, 1961, Conchita and Mary Cruz had two summonses, and yet they did not receive a third or enter a trance. Mary Loli and Jacinta, on the other hand, had a trance lasting six minutes at 5:50 p.m., in the course of which they gave the Virgin medals and rosaries to kiss.

During the afternoon of the 24th, Mary Cruz, in an ecstasy, asked through Conchita, who was not in a trance, if there was a priest present. She replied that there was one in street clothes. On descending from the pine grove, she was heard to say: "You want me to give the priest my hand, do you? You say he's walking down beside me?" Thereupon she grasped his hand and descended to the village in a trance at his side.

In her ecstasy of August 31st, Jacinta remarked aloud that the Virgin had told her that a priest was present, wearing his cassock tucked up beneath his trench-coat. The cleric was overcome with amazement. Stepping forward, he gave her his crucifix to offer to the Virgin. "This Crucifix comes from Rome; the Pope gave it to you," said Jacinta when she returned it to him. The priest confirmed this statement.

In an ecstasy on October 2nd, Mary Loli returned straight to its owner a medal kissed by the Virgin. It had intentionally been given to the visionary through three different people, so that there should remain no clue to whom it belonged. Nevertheless, she went to the right person without hesitation.

The same occurred with someone else, although this time in a far more spectacular fashion, because the child groped her way through the crowd, consulting the apparition until she found the owner.

No apparition took place on October 8th. Mary Loli was in bed with a heavy cold. Mary Cruz and Conchita were taken down to Cosio by car and returned late for the rosary at the church. Conchita asked Jacinta to beg the Blessed Virgin's forgiveness on her behalf, if she saw her, for having missed the rosary.

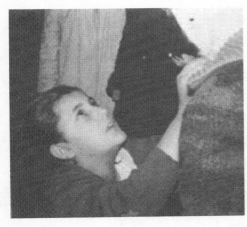

The girls return
the medals to
their owners.

"Work the miracle for those who believe."

48.—On September 1st, while in ecstasy, Conchita said: "How lovely the miracle is! How I wish you would work it soon! Why don't you! Do it just for those who believe; the people who don't believe don't mind anyhow!"

On October 16th, Mary Loli placed a wedding-ring on a woman's finger and, taking another, she worked her way through the onlookers until she faced a stranger who proved to be the husband of the lady who had handed the visionary the two rings.

In the course of the same trance, a stranger entered the house. It was his first visit to Garabandal. In his arms he bore an ailing child, convulsed with sobs. The visionary at once made her way towards the stranger and made a Sign of the Cross over the mite with her crucifix. The child instantly stopped crying and chuckled happily. Overcome with emotion, the father said: "I've never seen him smile until today." On emerging from her trance, Mary Loli asked after the sick child. "The Virgin said I was to tell you not to worry," she informed the parent. At that very moment, Jacinta arrived on the scene in an ecstasy. Inquiring for the same man, she gave him the same message of assurance from the Virgin.

That very day, a totally skeptical priest from Asturias arrived wearing street clothes. He watched one of the children approach him. She offered him a crucifix to kiss several times. "If this is genuine," he thought to himself, "let the child come to." In an instant the visionary emerged from her ecstasy, smiled at the priest and turned to go home. Hardly had she taken a few steps, when she again went into a trance. The priest then said to himself: "If you've just made the Sign of the Cross over me with your crucifix because I am a priest, I want you to prove it to me again, giving me the crucifix to kiss and crossing me several times." This was a thing that the visionary had not yet done to. anyone.

No sooner had this request formed in his mind than the child turned round, came to him, "smiled, and besides proffering me the crucifix to kiss, made the Sign of the Cross over me three times in succession."

Seeing some visitors giving the children photographs to be signed, the priest followed suit. To his great astonishment, a few moments later the photograph was returned to him with a dedication alluding to his priesthood, despite his lay garb.

On orders from the parish priest, the little girls asked the Vision why she sometimes appeared under different titles. The reply came back: "I am Mary, the Blessed Virgin, and there is but one Blessed Virgin."

On another occasion, Fr. Marichalar, who entertained doubts as to the supernatural cause of the happenings at Garabandal, drew near to the child who was then talking to the Vision. She was clearly heard to say: "Oh, Don Valentin believes less today, does he?" The parish priest was taken aback. He had not confided his doubts to anybody.

Conchita, in ecstasy, makes the Sign of the Cross.

Pre-arranging the Hour

49.—In an apparition during the first half of November, the Blessed Virgin told the children that, after Saturday the 18th of that month. they would not see her again until Saturday, January 13th. And so it came about.

A young French Jewess called Catherine went to Garabandal one day, accompanied by a Catholic friend who was giving her instruction in the Catholic Faith. Conchita asked her when she was to be baptized, to which Catherine replied that, since she was only nineteen years old, she intended to wait until she was twenty-one, because her parents would not grant her permission. At Catherine's request, Conchita recited the Hail Mary in Greek, and some phrases in French that she had been taught by the late Fr. Luis Andreu. That afternoon, everyone attended the rosary service. The children could not take their eyes off Catherine. They were quite nonplussed by her case. Afterwards, they went to Ceferino's, for Mary Loli was there and had already received one summons. Shortly before falling into a trance, the child went to her bedroom to fetch a bottle of holy water; this she had been advised to do in case the Vision was the devil. Asked how many summons they had received, Mary Loli and Jacinta answered: "Three minus a little bit." True enough, instants later they fell into an ecstasy.

"She isn't a Catholic, she isn't a Catholic . . . She's only nineteen . . . She hasn't been baptized yet . . ." they were heard to say to the Vision.

They started to offer the Vision the medals to be kissed. Jacinta sought in vain the one Catherine had given her. Mary Loli then drew the bottle of holy water from her pocket. Only a little was left; the rest had earlier been sprinkled round the floor of the room prior to the trance. Taking the bottle, Loli cast the water up into the air. Then it happened. The water seemed to hang for a moment, concentrated in a single bubble, suspended over Catherine. Then, it fell on her in a little shower, sprinkling nowhere but on her head. This phenomenon was connected with Catherine's delayed baptism. The children afterwards related that the Virgin had laughed when they told her they had brought the holy water in case it was the devil. And, when they mentioned Catherine, the Virgin instructed them to throw the contents of the bottle up in the air, and they would "see what would happen". As a result of this strange occurrence, and all she saw and heard at Garabandal, Catherine became a Catholic a few days later.

From November 1961, the apparitions became fewer and farther between. Now, however, the little girls knew in advance the exact date when they would next have a vision. Here, we quote a letter on the subject from Dr. Ortiz Perez of Santander:

"In the events at Garabandal, it is truly surprising to note the precision with which the visions have occurred, without there having been a single error in the dates forecast.

"In this respect, it is interesting to hear the visionaries' statement during one of our chats. 'When the Virgin announces that we shall see her, she never fails us. The same is not the case when we insistently beg her to come, although she does grant our request sometimes'.

"I myself have noticed the enormous yearning that they have often had to see the Blessed Virgin. 'Just think if she were to appear now!'; 'How I wish I could see her now . . . !' These utterances have been made in circumstances that were highly favorable for self-suggestion, yet their wishes in such cases have never materialized.

"I find these details interesting because they are proof of the absence of self-suggestion.

"I enclose the notes taken during our visit to San Sebastian de Garabandal on December 8th last. Maria Dolores declared that she would see her again on January 13th, Mary Cruz and Jacinta on the 16th, and Conchita on the 27th. When returning from saying the rosary in the sunken lane on December 9th, the latter remarked to my wife: 'What ages it seems till the 27th! After that I'll see her many times in succession!' This mention of 'many times in succession' leads us to assume that she was told this in the last vision, because until that day she had only mentioned the one on the 27th.

"I also enclose some data on the boy in Barcelona who seems to have been cured in such a surprising fashion. The data was taken down directly in a statement made by his family to the sergeant-major of the Civil Guard at Puentenansa."

When the girls go into an ecstasy, they fall to their knees in a flash with crushing force. A film recording the moment of entering an ecstasy has been examined in slow motion, photograph by photograph, but the fall itself is not to be seen on a single frame. In a split second they pass from a normal standing position to their kneeling in ecstasy. How is it, one may well ask, that they can fall onto jagged stones and yet not come to any harm, and show no sign of pain?

In one trance, Conchita walked through the streets of Garabandal on her knees. She was wearing long stockings. After the ecstasy, they were found to be undamaged, despite the roughness of the ground.

During her vision on January 27th, 1962, Conchita was given a medal and chain. The chain was locked with a safety-catch and was very tricky to unfasten. Conchita did not know how the catch worked. Finding that she was unable to open it, the child appealed to the Vision. "It's broken, I can't do it. You put it on for me . . ." The chain was in place in no time, although the visionary herself could not work the catch.

Without taking their eyes off the Vision, the girls return the medals to their owners.

Many have been the cases of medals kissed by the Virgin acquiring on occasions a curious luminosity, and of rosaries that have sometimes given off an unmistakable scent of roses.

Given their age and constitution, the children ought to have been exhausted, for the length and frequency of the trances was enough to have made them seriously ill. But, their appearance and behavior were proof of their glowing health.

"You didn't believe before, but now you do."

50.—A skeptic came to Garabandal. During one vision, he thought to himself: "For me to believe this, the child will have to take my rosary from its case and hand it to me."

The visionary at once approached him, handed him his rosary and, to everyone's astonishment, said, "You didn't believe before, but now you do."

A lady asked Maria Dolores whether the Blessed Virgin was sad. "The Virgin can't be sad, because she's in heaven," the child replied.

"I know that," the woman insisted, "but, I mean, is she sad because of the sins of the world?"

"We're all sad because of *them*," came the reply! Who can put such answers on their lips?

It does not fall within our scope to go into all the cases of inexplicable cures and private miracles that are claimed to have been worked, because personal opinions exert too great an influence on such accounts. Let us simply say that many prodigies have already been attributed to Our Lady of Garabandal. Among these, according to his doctors and relatives, is the surprising cure of a son of Don Antonio Soldevilla. And that of Don Juan Fontanillas Buj, a seventeen-year old youth who was taken to San Pablo Hospital in Barcelona on October 5th in a critical condition following a motorcycle crash. He did not recover consciousness until the 14th. That day, he underwent two operations to no avail. His mother was informed that he would in all likelihood die. That night, a crucifix kissed by the Virgin was placed round his neck. In the early morning of the 15th, he awoke in a perfectly normal condition, and his injuries had healed. Equally marvelous was the alleged cure of Antonio Salcedo Fornall, of Chiclana de la Frontera. But, we cannot make it the aim of this book to delve into such delicate matters, for they are quite beyond our scope.

The visionaries have a great spirit of penitence, which is their interpretation of the teachings of the Vision. They used to rise at six o'clock each morning to say the rosary in the sunken lane. They did penance by placing dry pine needles in their shoes; they walked barefoot over thorns, etc. As a rule, phenomena resulting from hysteria take place under far more comfortable circumstances.

One night, a party arrived from Santander. Among them was an artist who showed Maria Dolores a medal that he had designed. "There's a painter, here," she said to the Vision. "He wants to know if you look all right on this medal . . . They make you look so ugly in all the holy pictures! And in fact you're so pretty . . . ! Eh? You say it's all right . . . ?"

The painter, who was standing close beside the visionary, was visibly overjoyed.

One of the reports written by Senorita Ascension de Luis, dated March 18th, 1962, reads as follows:

"Loli left Jacinta's house still in ecstasy and walked all round the village saying the rosary. Her gait seemed quite normal, and yet those of us who were following her had to run to keep up. In this fashion, she proceeded to the sunken lane, where the stony ground proves difficult to negotiate. The child went up the lane and descended again backwards at an incredible speed."

In another report, on May 9th, 1962, a canon from one of the Catalonian

This is the lane where "the child in ecstasy went up... and descended again backwards at an incredible speed"

dioceses made the following statement:

"On Easter Sunday, Don Valentin asked the Lord to make him see clearly, once and for all, whether or not the apparition of the Virgin to the children was true. As proof, he asked that, if it was true, the children should come to him in ecstasy that very night while he was asleep, wake him up, make the Sign of the Cross over him and give him the crucifix to kiss. And so it came about that, shortly after two o'clock in the morning, one of the visionaries came in a trance to the door of the house where Don Valentin was staying the night, and started to knock at the door. As all the inmates were in bed, at first nobody answered. But, so violently did the child persist in her knocking, that the door was eventually opened. Don Valentin was still fast asleep, unaware that the child was in the house. Still in ecstasy, she reached the parish priest's bedroom. There, without any warning knock, she entered and pressed her crucifix to his lips until he awoke with a start. The child proceeded to make the Sign of the Cross over him several times with the crucifix, smiled sweetly at him and left the room."

"Fr. Marichalar was 'punished'—as the same report puts it—by the Apostolic Administrator, the Auxiliary Bishop of Santander, for a period of two months, because he was thought to be the originator of the goings-on at Garabandal. This in itself, is to my mind, one of the most convincing points in favor of the supernatural cause of these events."

Some most impressive letters were written by Conchita in her awkward scrawling handwriting, replying on Our Lady's behalf to petitions made to her in prayer, without the visionary knowing anything about them, but simply fulfilling her mission as a messenger.

There is also the surprising case of the conversion of a Protestant, Don Maximo Foerschler, of Madrid. Here is a short quotation from the letter he himself wrote to Don Rafael Fontaneda Perez on March 29th, 1962: "The reason I am writing to you is so that you may share my great joy, for, next Sunday, God willing, I shall join the Catholic Church like all of you and receive Holy Communion from Fr. Ramon Andreu, a Jesuit priest[†] after a quiet baptism in private.

"This is all I have to tell you, and I do so much moved and with the utmost joy."

Peculiarities of Certain Trances

51.—When the children went into an ecstatic trance with some object still clutched in their hands, it often proved impossible to make them relinquish their grasp or to pull it away from them. The same was true if they had a hold on somebody's arm. They continued to cling to that arm during the ecstasy, even when walking along, and forcing the owner to kneel down or walk by their side throughout.

On March 17th, 1962, Mary Loli gave the Vision several articles to kiss, among others a reliquary belonging to the Marques de Santa Maria and his wife, who are fortunate enough to have been present during a great many of the visionaries' mystical phenomena. The reliquary contained what was thought to be a splinter of the True Cross, but there were doubts as to its authenticity. The Vision confirmed that it had belonged to the True Cross. Mary Loli then made as though to give the Vision the Marquesa de Santa Maria's wedding-ring, but, instead of removing it from the latter's finger, she

---

[†] Fr. Ramon Andreu is the brother of Fr. Luis, who died when returning home from Garabandal. Four of the Andreu brothers were Jesuits. The three still alive can be seen in a photograph in the company of the author.

took her hand and raised it to the Vision's lips, twisting the ring round so that she might kiss every part of it.

On the Feast of St. Joseph, Mary Loli began to write on a slip of paper while in an ecstasy. She shielded the piece of paper from view with her hand so that nobody should see it: "To Don José a Happy Feast Day from Loli". The Don José in question was a stranger, a priest who had arrived at Garabandal that day without saying a word to anyone. Then, taking a holy picture, she wrote: "To Don José, with best wishes from the Virgin". While she was writing this note, her father covered her eyes to prove to everybody that she could not see what she was doing.

In a report dated April 15th, 1962, which I have in front of me as I write, a witness says: "Four of us stayed on at Conchita's, a priest, another cleric who had come in street clothes, the youth who had accompanied them, and a friend of mine. The young man inquired of Conchita whether she had remembered to ask the Virgin for a reply to the three questions to which he had requested an answer. 'Yes, I asked her,' Conchita replied, 'but the Virgin told me to answer you by letter when you write to me, because it isn't three things that you want the answer to, but more.' Her audience were taken aback. 'How many?' the youth inquired. 'Five,' came the reply. Conchita herself had no idea of these questions. My friend told me the story as a clear example of conscience reading, despite the fact that he is most guarded, when it comes to asserting things that have no natural explanation."

His report continues. "During her ecstasy, Mary Loli made the Sign of the Cross over all those present. One of our number, who had already

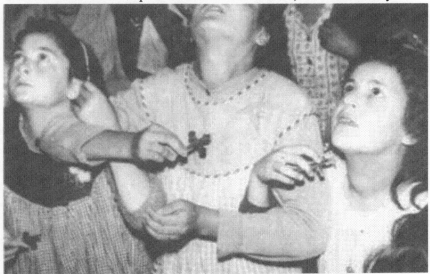

"When in ecstasy, light falling in their eyes does not cause them to blink" (See text)

been crossed, changed his position, and when the little girl came to him a second time, she passed him by."

MORE VIEWS

of

the girls in ecstasy

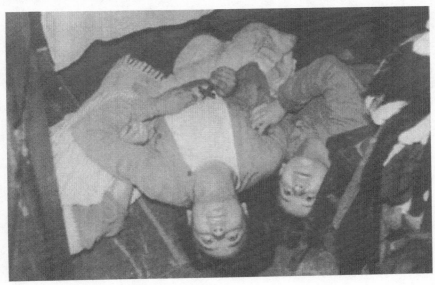

The prodigies at Garabandal have brought about countless conversions and awakened not a few vocations.

At the Vision's behest, the children asked for a shrine to be built in the pine grove and dedicated to St. Michael, for it was he who appeared to them in the beginning and prepared the children for their Visions of Our Blessed Lady.

When in ecstasy, light falling on their eyes does not cause them to blink. This can be appreciated in a film taken under bright arc-lights which made no impression on the visionaries at all. But, on emerging from their trance, they could be seen to react immediately, shielding their eyes from the unbearable glare.

Let us end this chapter by recalling the case of a visitor who was wedged in the farthest corner of the house where the children were in a trance. The visitor inwardly formed a request. "If my confessions hitherto have been good, let the child come to me and offer me her crucifix to kiss." No sooner thought than done. One of the visionaries left her companions and shuffled across on her knees, in a trance, to the person in question.

I think these brief details help to complete the picture, giving added depth to the prodigies that we are examining.

Padre Pio in conversation with Carlos Campanini, an Italian television actor, who witnessed the ecstasy of June 18, 1965

Chapter Eight

OTHER TESTIMONIES

52.—A group of Spaniards once asked Padre Pio whether the happenings at San Sebastian de Garabandal were true. They declare that the Capuchin monk retorted in his customary harsh voice: "Are you still asking about that? How long do you expect her to appear there? She has been appearing for eight months already!"

On March 3rd, 1962, Conchita received a typewritten letter in Italian. It was unsigned and bore no indication as to the sender's address; the postmark was blurred and illegible. The letter referred to the little girls as "the blessed children of San Sebastian de Garabandal", affirming the authenticity of their visions of the Blessed Virgin, and finished: "I can only give you one piece of advice: *pray and make others pray;* because the world is at the threshold of its perdition. People do not believe in you or in your conversations with the White Lady, but they will believe when it is too late."

According to Conchita, she asked the Blessed Virgin who had sent the letter, and the Vision confirmed that it was from Padre Pio. The visionary hastened to send off her reply.

"Everything to do with Garabandal occurs under the Virgin's influence, and there is nothing natural or diabolical about it." This is how Fr. Corta ends an article published in "Estrella del Mar."

"I have not been to Heaven, but I have been to Garabandal, which is the gates of Heaven," states an eminent and saintly theologian.

Likewise, after witnessing the ecstasies that took place at Garabandal, a priest who has written some searching works on mystical phenomena said: "Though I am not infallible, as a specialist in these matters, I can assert the supernatural causes which, to my mind, are to be found in the phenomena that I have witnessed."[†]

The Opinions of Doctors

53.—A leading Madrid specialist forbade his medical staff to ridicule events at Garabandal. He informed them that there was no explanation for these phenomena, and that they deserve the closest attention and great respect.

[†] At the time of sending this manuscript to press, it was considered advisable to omit the names of some witnesses, in view of the impossibility of obtaining permission from all of them in time.

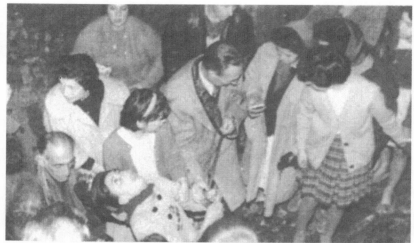
Dr. Ortiz checks Conchita's pulse during an ecstasy

In a letter dated February 2nd, a pediatrician writes: "The point that still draws my attention is that, after seven consecutive months of marvelous ecstatic trances, the children are still, in my opinion, absolutely normal, although many people, even without seeing for themselves, maintain that it is all due to pathological causes."

In his report on February 26th, 1962, the same specialist proceeds as follows:

"What a strange disease! One which is announced days or months in advance. In childhood, mental disorders of all kinds present characteristic symptoms which are: continual lethargy, troubled sleep, aggressiveness of character and an uncontrollable outward anxiety. After eight consecutive months of this, not only do they not show any of these symptoms, but quite the opposite."

Mary-Loli as she normally appears in everyday life.

"I found the children happy, and their parents tell me that they sleep like logs; they are especially sweet-natured, are still obedient and show a spirit of unlimited submission. So, in my view, they are still as normal as ever."

The same doctor drew up a long medical report in October, 1962. We shall not quote it in full owing to its length and highly technical nature, but the report ends with the following conclusions:

"1. From the pediatric and psychiatric viewpoints, the four girls have always been, and still are, quite normal.

2. Their ecstatic trances cannot be classified in any of the physiological or psychopathological patterns known today.

3. Given the length of time that these phenomena have been occurring, if they had been due to pathological causes of any kind, easily proven symptoms would have made their appearance.

4. Within the field of both normal and pathological child psychology, I can find no explanation whatsoever that might throw some natural light on a series of phenomena that clearly escape the bounds of the natural order."

He sums up his opinion as follows: "Our enormous pride collapses when God confronts us with one of these dilemmas to show us how limited the possibilities of medicine are. Any attempt to explain away a phenomenon that is largely 'irrational' by purely rational means is both absurd and doomed to failure."

In the December 1962 issue of "Gaceta Medica Espanola", the magazine of the Spanish medical profession. Dr. Antonio Castillo Lucas published an article called "Memories of last summer in the mountains of Santander, from a medical point of view". In this article, after studying everything he had seen, he wound up by saying: "I feel that we doctors should undertake a scientific study of the phenomenon, and of the attendant circumstances of isolation, heredity, consanguinity and other elements, for we consider the mental health of these little girls to be in jeopardy, what with the present atmosphere of expectation and curiosity, complicated interrogation, theorizing and other psychological factors that tend to disturb their peace of mind and that of their relatives; and we consider that this situation could end in collective neurosis."

I find this attitude quite reasonable, although the fact is that the girls live peacefully in spite of everything, and daily show their perfect mental balance.

On February 25th, 1965, Dr. Ricardo Puncernau, a neuropsychiatrist from Barcelona, gave a lecture on "The facts of Garabandal, as seen by a doctor". In his talk, he tackled the subject from a doctor's angle.

Dr. Puncernau knows the case well, having studied it very thoroughly, spending long periods with the children and paying the closest attention to the analysis of all their reactions. At the end of his lecture, he declared: "I believe these happenings are of the greatest scientific interest and consequently deserve further, serious investigation. The truth of the matter is that no natural explanation can be found to cover them as a whole, so that, thus far, from a strictly scientific point of view, there is no denying the possibility of a supernatural cause behind all these phenomena. In the light of this possibility, it would be illogical from a Christian point of view to adopt a disdainful attitude."[†]

In his lecture, Dr. Puncernau merely ratified his thorough report of November 10th, 1962, which we cannot quote in full here owing to its length and technical nature. However, it ends as follows: "With the facts standing as they are, it is difficult for a doctor to find a purely natural explanation; one that would be easily understandable in itself, fully satisfactory and cover all the facts. Hence, as men of science, we must continue our examination of the extraordinary phenomena at Garabandal and hope to collect fresh data."

Finally, we have Dr. Alejandro Gasca Ruiz, who was working in Santander at the time of the apparitions. He was present during a great many of these inexplicable events, and has drawn up a cautious report signed jointly by himself and Dr. Ortiz Gonzalez. The main points made in the document are the following:

"Although we realize how little our modest knowledge can contribute to clarifying matters, our having followed and studied the events closely puts us under the obligation to express our opinion, for not to do so would be an act of rank scientific cowardice.

"For three consecutive years, we have personally kept an eye on the ecstatic phenomena at San Sebastian de Garabandal and their protagonists. Two features have struck us as members of the medical profession: 1. The total psychosomatic normality of the children, both then and now, in spite of having been subjected for long hours to a state of unconsciousness. 2. The fact that the four children's ecstatic trances have been accompanied by a series of parapsychological phenomena such as telepathy, premonitions, clairvoyance, retrovisions, hierognosis, falls while in ecstatic walks, levitation in the case of one child; namely, a great number of phenomena that are today classified as extra sensory perception.

"Consequently, we should have to admit, in all four children, such a degree of parapsychological ability that it would embrace

---

[†] Quoted from the newspaper report on Dr. Puncernau's lecture.

"Consequently, we should have to admit, in all four children, such a degree of parapsychological ability that it would embrace most forms of extra sensory perception. Is this not a veritable scientific miracle? Let us remember the study undertaken in this respect by the London Institute of Parapsychology in cooperation with the radio and television networks. Out of eight million inhabitants tested, how few subjects showed signs of any of these faculties! In no case did the subject possess more than one faculty.

"Today, man cannot subject, control and implement the unconscious zone of his mental faculties in the same way that he can make use of his conscious zone.

"We cannot find any convincing scientific solution to explain such phenomena.

"Other doctors prefer to wait, in the light of the miracle announced by the children, shielded by their attitude of doubt and their impotence to explain the prodigies; but, let it not be forgotten that, more often than not, doubts imply a tragic form of belief."

A Newspaper Article on Garabandal

54.—The *"Pensamiento Alaves"*, in its number of April 27th, 1962, ran an interesting article by Dr. Jose de la Vega, telling of his visit to San Sebastian de Garabandal. I think it is only appropriate to quote a newspaper report in this chapter devoted to the testimony written by others. It reads as follows:

"Since June 18th last, the Blessed Virgin has been walking almost daily through the twisting streets of a little village way up among the Cantabrian peaks. This is the claim of four little girls between the ages of ten and twelve, born and bred in the heart of the Santander uplands and devoid of any schooling other than the lessons taught them by the parish priest."

"The entire village, with its bare seventy families, has been in a state of confusion for months. Once, or even several times, each day, at pre-arranged hours, the children pray with, talk and blow kisses to the Virgin Mary, while lost in a deep ecstatic trance. The poor families of these children are frightened.

"The Church has prudently refrained from giving an opinion. Even the most incredulous doctors finally admit that the goings-on defy logical explanation. But, day after day, thousands of believers hailing from distant parts arrive at the hamlet, fervent in their faith and tears of emotion in their eyes; and in their faith they find the sole explanation of this extraordinary series of occurrences that is lived over and over, night after night, in San Sebastian de Garabandal.

"I spent Holy Week among these people. I lent an ear to villagers and visitors alike; I chatted with the children before and after their visions. Since, professionally speaking, I can find no explanation for what I saw, I feel bound to believe in a prodigy.

"'Did you see the Blessed Virgin,' people ask me.

"'No, I didn't,' I confess, 'but I did feel her presence in my heart and soul.'

"Doctor, I find you most skeptical," remarked a Jesuit Father who accompanied me.

"No, Father. It's not that," I responded. "I'm utterly disconcerted. My dearest wish would be to feel just as the children and everybody else feel about it. But, you know far better than I do that faith is a gift that God doesn't give us all in the same measure."

"A few hours later, I found myself watching the second apparition at close quarters. It was before dawn on Holy Saturday. The rain was pouring down, and the whole village looked like a rock-strewn mud-pie. Armed with torches, we followed one of the visionaries at a great pace as she went round the village streets in ecstasy. Clasped between her hands was a crucifix. Her head was thrown back, her smiling eyes staring up at the heavens . . . From time to time, she would drop to her knees, pray and kiss the Cross. Half the locals and all the strangers, even visiting children, followed her, open-mouthed in wonder. Only shortly beforehand, in her humble peasant kitchen—where she had spoken to us rather drowsily, for it was 4 a.m.—we had seen her suddenly fall into an. ecstatic trance, falling to her knees without burning herself on the searing stones of the blazing hearth. As though uplifted by angels' wings, she rose to her feet and commenced her tour of the village. Stumbling in the pitch blackness of the night, spattering one another with mud up to our eyebrows, we pursued her, never pausing for breath.

"Fervently, I begged God to grant me the grace of faith.

"In the little visionary's wake, we plunged down practically every lane and alley in the hamlet; we visited the church porch, the cemetery, and the mountainside where the Virgin Mary had appeared for the first time.

"The unevenness of the ground underfoot, the darkness and my city-dweller's innate clumsiness caused me to trip up on every stone that lay in my path. Bit by bit, I was left behind. I could go no farther and decided to await the return of the others. My wife could not bear to stop, despite the fact that she was already panting for breath. On she went, drawing courage from my own incredulity.

"All of a sudden, before she reached the brow, the ecstatic child halted in her tracks and started to run downhill backwards, scarcely brushing the steep stony ground in her passage, her smiling gaze never leaving the night sky. Reaching the spot where I was waiting, she stopped. With a resounding thud, she fell to her bare knees on the sharp stones, as though they were a feather cushion. Then, she raised her crucifix heavenwards, paused, and proffered it to me to kiss. Around her neck were hanging medals and rosaries belonging to nearly all those present. Her fingers sought a particular chain, while she whispered rather than talked to her invisible apparition:

" 'Tell me which one it is. Is this it?' She held the medal up for the Virgin in her vision to kiss. 'Now, tell me whose it is,' we all heard her murmur huskily.

"Without a moment's hesitation, she turned to my wife, opened the gold catch of the chain and fastened it round her neck. My wife fell to her knees, moved to tears like myself and others who saw that strange scene. The child made her kiss the medal blessed by the Virgin Mary's lips and helped her to her feet with an angelic smile that we shall never forget.

"In like fashion, with roughly the same words, she placed round my neck my own medal kissed by Our Blessed Lady. I could no longer contain my emotion and dropped to my knees, too, with the sting of tears on my cheeks.

"At that instant, I discovered the explanation of all that I had thus far not understood. In the heavenly expression on that child's face, I saw reflected the invisible presence of Our Lady of Mount Carmel overhead. I wept unashamedly on my knees, and begged God's forgiveness for my incredulity.

"Like everybody else who goes there for a first time, I must go back to San Sebastian de Garabandal. With me I shall take doctors and friends, and I shall ask them to try to explain the prodigy of those four little girls from the uplands of Santander. But, with all my heart, I beg God never to let them take away from me the emotion I experienced that night. It is so beautiful to believe in the miracle!"

An Authoress's Account

55.—We cannot overlook Spanish literary circles in this chapter written by others.

Here is an extract from the moving pages about her visit to Garabandal by the brilliant Catalonian authoress, Mercedes Salisachs.

"Holy Saturday, April 21st, 1962.

I must confess, although I do not consider myself especially gullible where prodigies are concerned, no more do I feel bound to discount them simply on ethical grounds or on established principle. Many have been the 'gifts' that God has sent mankind in the course of the centuries. True enough, our faith should not be based on such 'gifts', but, if they are genuine, there is nothing to prevent our making use of them to nourish our religious life.

And this was really what I was looking for when I first set out for the village of Garabandal. I wanted to come closer to God and render homage to the Virgin Mary, although, naturally enough, I still had doubts as to the authenticity of the alleged apparitions.

The fact is that my religious life had undergone a considerable change some three and a half years earlier, as a result of the death of my son Miguel, and following an inner crisis that had entirely swept aside the deep-rooted habits and theories of a life-time.

Although I was a practicing Catholic, it was from force of habit and a sense of duty rather than from love of God.

My son, Miguel, on the other hand, was religious in the "spiritual" sense. The firmness of his faith was astonishing; especially the maturity of his reasoning. Without being a mystic, everything he did and thought had an underlying religious purpose, perhaps in contrast with the human effort that any of his ventures entailed.

His artistic work, praised by all the Spanish press following posthumous exhibitions in Madrid and Barcelona, give only a glimpse of the quasi-mystical spirituality which was reflected in his conversation and habits. The final result of his life, however, fully confirmed the greatness of his soul.

He was engaged when he died, and had intended getting married when he was twenty-two. With this in mind, he had done his military service earlier than usual. There was nothing in him to suggest the end he was to meet. Bursting with health, ever making new plans, he was the living embodiment of the future. Yet, on more than one occasion I had heard him exclaim forlornly: 'I'm wasting my time. The years are catching up with me . . .' He seemed goaded to these outbursts by something that neither he nor anyone comprehended. Seeing his disquiet Ent, I would do what I could to calm him: 'But, you've got your whole life before you.' But, his 'fear' of not accomplishing what he planned to do was stronger than any reasoning: 'I haven't a minute to lose ... I must gain time . . .'

All the same, I think his sense of urgency was unconscious. At any rate, I never heard him mention the slightest suspicion of what fate had in store for him. Yet, his maturity was becoming increasingly apparent. The last year of his life was marvelous. The metaphysical evolution he was undergoing was very noticeable. He had succeeded in correcting his own inclination to rebelliousness to such a degree that, if ever it rose to the surface through ill-humor, he at once burst out laughing. 'There's nothing so grotesque as a rage', he used to say. Consequently, his company was a tonic to everybody, and conversation with him was a blessing.

About a month before he died, he and his fiancee decided (I think in fulfillment of a thanksgiving resolution) to receive Holy Communion every day. This new habit, which he never mentioned to me, but which I suspected, accentuated to an even greater degree the signs of his self-control; he had acquired an enviable calm, and his stoicism in adversity was uncommon at his age.

Indeed, adversity crossed his path on not a few occasions. In spite of the apparent ease of his life, year after year, difficulties beset him at every step. It is incredible how many of his ventures were doomed by adversity.

Towards the end, however, he no longer seemed to care about the mounting obstacles that barred his path. He gave the impression that, as far as he was concerned, nothing could really be adverse again. Shortly before his death, he exclaimed to a friend of his: 'I've been to Communion twenty days running. What a fool I am for not having done it before!' And he slapped his hand to his head in exasperation.

On October 30th, 1958, after going to Communion as usual, he set off for France with four fellow artists. Ten kilometers from their goal, they had an accident. Two of them were killed instantaneously. Two survived.

Miguel died at six o'clock the following morning, the 31st. I do not think he would have recovered consciousness.

I have given this short account, because the things that happened to me at San Sebastian de Garabandal are closely connected with it.

I have no idea what other mothers can have felt at the loss of a son like Miguel. But, I doubt whether they can have overcome the same sort of emptiness and horror that engulfed me. Our understanding of each other was such that, when speaking of him to me before his death, even his brothers and sisters (to say nothing of his friends) did not bother to mention him by name. They simply said 'our son', as though he were the only one.

Everyone considered Miguel as my *alter ego,* my real confidant and inseparable companion. They were not mistaken.

In our spare time, the three of us (his fiancée, he and I) were wont to get together. We went out together, or else stayed at home, chatting. His whims were always the same as mine and our plans were always made together. For my part, having him at my side was like owning a piece of cosmos. On him I focused all my good aspirations, and I believe he had the same attitude towards me. In fact, he was not just my son, but my best friend, too.

So, it is hardly surprising that his death should have snuffed out the main point in my life, and that, on losing him, I should have felt overwhelmed by the most horrifying, stygian gloom.

People told me that I would get over it in time; that, although I would not manage to forget him, memory of him would gradually fade until he became a pleasant recollection. People said that, little by little, I would get used to not seeing him, not hearing his voice, and that I would eventually accept matters without such a wrench.

But, time went by, and I was still desperate. Although I attempted to hide my sadness, especially so as not to hurt the feelings of my other four children, the more time passed the emptier, sadder and more lost I felt.

Some resorted to religious reasoning. They spoke to me of Christian resignation, reminded me of Miguel's great faith, of his exemplary death, and said I should praise God for having taken him from me with his soul in such happy circumstances. But, resignation would not come, and all their persuasion struck me as empty, thoughtless arguments.

There even came a time when doubts about my faith became my obsession. Religion took on the appearance of a repair-patch on a burst tire, and everything that I had hitherto admitted without undue effort now started to crumble, plunging me into greater and greater depression. In this fashion, I finally turned into an empty shell with no horizon but the past, and no hope for the future but death.

The collapse of my morale was shattering. The temptation to 'doubt' continually assailed me. I got the impression that after death everything was over, that hope was nothing but a great lie, and that faith was a childish myth invented to keep us in order.

My doubts, however, did not win completely. Sometimes, for some unknown reason, hope returned. 'What if Miguel can see me? What if the dogma of the Communion of Saints is true . . . ?' It was as if Miguel were tugging at me; as if he were screaming out to me to arouse me from my apathy.

At that period, I could not even pray. I always ran into a blank wall of doubt. On one occasion, I remember, my mother suggested we should all say the rosary together, and (I still feel ashamed at my retort) I refused because I considered it 'vulgar'.

The fact was, I needed some proof; something to make me realize that, beyond death's threshold, life continued. But proof was not forthcoming, and, to tell the truth, I did not do anything to seek it out either. My devotion to Our Blessed Lady was practically non-existent.

One day, shortly before the feast of the Immaculate Conception, almost instinctively I found myself before a statue of Our Lady of Sorrows, begging the Blessed Virgin to give me proof that Miguel indeed existed still.

Proof was not long in coming. It was indisputable evidence. So incontestable was it that, even if someone were now to explain it away with normal arguments, I should still be convinced that what happened was nevertheless an answer from Our Lady.

From that day onwards, I had no other obsession than to return to God. Five months later (on May 4th, 1959, to be exact), I made a general confession and my peace with God, once and for all, resolving never to part from Him for a single second of my remaining life.

From that moment, everything began to change for me. Though I still missed Miguel greatly, and loneliness continued to torment me, my inward peace was now a great balm.

Reciting the rosary ceased to strike me as 'vulgar', and my devotion to the Virgin Mary grew day by day.

So it was that, when I heard of the children of Garabandal, I made up my mind to visit their little village, not just out of curiosity, but with the idea of rendering homage to the Virgin, even though the authenticity of the phenomena might be debatable.

My First Trip

Taking advantage of the fact that the family was away in Switzerland at the time, I left Barcelona on Maundy Thursday (1962), accompanied by our chauffeur, Jose, and his wife, Mercedes. We reached Cosio at noon on Good Friday.

In Cosio, I met the parish priest of Garabandal, Don Valentin Marichalar. While waiting for the car that was to drive us up to the village, I had an opportunity of speaking to him. He struck me as a kindly man, intelligent yet simple. As far as I could make out, his position was a very awkward one. Obedience to his superiors obliged him to be stern about the prodigies, and this severity was not always taken with good grace by his parishioners.

Despite his caution, he ended up by confessing that, at heart, he was convinced that the phenomenon occurring there was supernatural, and that their innocence made the little girls worthy to receive the visits of the Virgin.

He also spoke to me of the outstanding moral uprightness of the villagers, their religious fervor and a long-standing custom of saying the rosary in the village church every evening, even when he himself was away.

This chat with the village priest heightened my curiosity to meet the children. It was 2 p.m. when the car that was to take us turned up. Fidel, the driver, informed us that Fr. Corta, a Jesuit who had come to help Fr. Marichalar with the Holy Week ceremonies, was then about to give Holy Communion. The village *en masse* had congregated in the church.

From time to time, the children passed close to us. They appeared to be on very friendly terms with the Santa Marias, through whom I managed to get introduced to the private circle of each one.

That afternoon, I entrusted Jacinta with some pious objects to give to the Virgin to kiss. I made her and her fellow visionaries the same request: 'Ask the Virgin for news of my son.' I think it was Jacinta who inquired: 'What's wrong with your son?' I told her he had died.

This done, I made my way to Mary Loli's, where everyone was waiting for her next apparition. I gave Mary Loli a sheet of paper written on both sides. On handing it to her, I told her that I did not expect an answer. 'The only thing I should like to know is where my son is.' I did not mention his name. The one who might have known it was Jacinta, since I had left a commemoration card of his on the table for the Virgin to kiss. Jacinta might quite feasibly have informed Mary Loli secretly, but it does not seem in keeping for Mary Loli to lie when she told me that the name 'Miguel' was given her by the Virgin.

I still did not know how the visions occurred. Though they had been explained to me, I found it difficult to visualize them. I have now been to Garabandal three times and have seen many ecstasies, yet I still think there is no way of describing, not just the visionaries' "fall", their facial expressions and movements, but the atmosphere of respect that always reigns supreme when 'the apparitions arrive', in spite of the background of some of the tourists and the villagers' familiarity with these events.

A few days ago, I asked the children whether they had got accustomed to the idea of seeing the Blessed Virgin. Mary Loli came out with a very subtle reply. 'At this minute, I feel as if I have got accustomed now; but, when I see her again, it's as if it was something new.'

Well, that is in fact precisely the case with those of us who are present during an ecstasy. We feel as if we were already used to them; but, on seeing them afresh, we are still overcome with surprise.

At first sight, nothing that the children do appears to have any point to it. Their movements, their swaying motions, their headlong running, their conversations in an undertone, their insistence when proffering the crucifix in their hands for people to kiss . . . All these factors at first leave the onlooker open-mouthed in wonder at their incongruence and apparent inconsistence. (There is a priest who stated in his report that the goings-on at Garabandal were 'hardly dignified', most likely overlooking the scant dignity at Lourdes).

Even admitting the undignified appearance of events, nothing that occurs there occurs without a purpose. The trouble is that, to grasp this, you have to stay in the village at least three days. Once you are acquainted with the apparent incongruence, everything is clear. Whether instantaneously or belatedly, the explanation is always forthcoming.

I, for my part, ought to add that, although my yearning was great, my hope was weak. I had approached my trip the same way one does a pilgrimage. I was prepared to put up with any discomforts or obstacles.

It was not long before we heard the characteristic thud of Mary Loli falling to her knees. It came from upstairs. Silence fell and only a short time had elapsed when we saw Mary Loli descending the stairs, her eyes staring heavenwards and her face transfigured, holding hands with another little girl.

I do not think the greatest actress could imitate that expression.

Mary Loli went to the table on which lay the objects to be presented to the Virgin. She began to hold them aloft to be kissed. I saw her pick up my sheet of paper, raise it on high, turn it round and deposit it on the table once more.

Then, clutching her crucifix, she went out into the street. Her regular strides were light and easy. It was as though she were walking on a smooth, flat surface. She was unaware of the quagmires, puddles, rubble and stones underfoot ...

Somehow or other, I grabbed the arm of the child to whom she was clinging, but, after a halt at the church door, Mary Loli started up the mountainside and I was forced to relinquish my hold. Exhaustion prevented my following them any farther. I felt as though my galloping heart beats would give out at any moment, so steep was the slope leading up to the pine grove.

Thus far, the evening had been none too pleasant as far as I was concerned. Often though the child had given the Cross to be kissed, she had overlooked me. I was deeply pained by the suspicion that, if all this was true, the Virgin Mary was deliberately evading my kiss.

When Mary Loli at last started down the mountainside, I saw her running backwards, her gaze piercing the gloom overhead, avoiding obstacles and pot holes as if she had eyes in the back of her head. When she reached the village, she was joined by Jacinta; they laughed as they met. . . Both of them proffered their crucifixes for people to kiss and walked on arm in arm.

At the church door, Jacinta emerged from her trance. Mary Loli returned home, still in a state of ecstasy.

I called Jacinta to me and asked for news of Miguel. The child replied that the Virgin had not answered her query. Downcast, I tackled Mary Loli next. Her response was identical. "Did she read my sheet of paper?" I urged. "Yes, she read it."

Realizing my disappointment, Fr. Corta inquired when she would see Our Lady again. "From two o'clock to half past two," she said. Fr. Corta suggested that she should once more ask the Virgin for news of my son when she saw her again.

That same night, when Mary Loli fell into an ecstatic trance for the second time, she was joined at once by Jacinta who was walking around the streets in a trance, too. Again, they gave all the onlookers their crucifixes to kiss; again, when they came my way, they passed my lips by.

But the worst of all was what they told me on re-emerging. Both Jacinta and Mary Loli told me the same story. "The Blessed Virgin gave me her answer, but I can't tell you what it is."

That reply was far worse than the previous one. There was no escaping the obvious conclusions. Either I did not deserve to be answered by the Virgin, or else, despite every supposition to the contrary, Miguel was in a place of which it was "better to remain in ignorance".

I goaded Mary Loli to tell me whether the Virgin's answer was pleasant or otherwise. "I can't say, I can't say . . ." she evaded my questioning. Her face was quite inscrutable.

Fr. Corta again tried to come to my rescue. He saw I was upset, and doubtless felt sorry for me. "Can you tell her tomorrow?" The child shrugged. "Perhaps ..."

Going to bed that night, I felt as if I had been turned into a block of ice. The suspicion that neither God nor Our Blessed Mother wanted to have anything to do with me depressed me as much as my assumption that Miguel might be suffering punishment. But, somehow it seemed out of the question to doubt Miguel's salvation ..

I wondered whether my conscience was, perhaps, not as clear as it might be. Yet, much as I tried to probe it and discover some grievous sin, I could recall nothing. I told myself that maybe the Virgin wanted me to show greater piety, more care when reciting the rosary, more humility . . .
One by one, I re-examined the phenomena that I had witnessed throughout that day and night. I desired with all my heart to discover a "flaw", grounds to disprove their authenticity . . . something that would make me see clearly that what was happening in Garabandal was sheer mumbo-jumbo. But, the more I

went over the facts in my mind, the more authentic everything seemed. The only flaw in the whole set-up was myself. That was undoubtedly why the Virgin did not want me to kiss the crucifix.

Holy Saturday was a barren day, too. Notwithstanding the kindness shown me by the Santa Marias, Fr. Corta, Fr. Marichalar, the sergeant-major of the Civil Guard and even the mothers of the visionaries, everything in the village seemed hostile to me. Their kindness was no doubt due to the pity and distrust awakened in them by the isolation to which the Virgin had sentenced me. To me, it was of no importance at all what people might be thinking. What hurt me most was that continual disdain.

It was then that I first began to have a presentiment that everything that was happening to me was sheer trickery, a sort of trap ... I remembered that it was Holy Week. Could all this have something to do with the liturgy? I hardly dared think so; it seemed too subtle, too easy a way out. . .

But, the fact is, with the coming of that presentiment, I lost all notion of fear. I accepted everything and submitted to God's will.

That night, I had supper alone in the tavern. Afterwards, the sergeant-major of the Civil Guard took me round to Conchita's house.

Conchita's mother welcomed me kindly and offered me a seat next to her daughter. The heat of the fire on the hearth was bothersome, and I began to feel increasingly uncomfortable. But, as the hours passed, my morale gradually revived.

We chatted of this and that, of things that were not particularly closely connected with the visions. The most striking thing about those children is their naturalness in everyday life. They accept the supernatural with almost incredible simplicity. They feel that anyone can "see the Virgin", and that what is happening to them is perfectly normal.

What really worries them is to see people's disbelief. Over and over again, they ask people, "Do you believe? Do you really believe I see the Virgin?" They probably think that it depends on that belief whether or not the Virgin works the great miracle that she has been announcing from the very first. Conchita is particularly prone to this worry. When least expected, there she is asking, "Do you believe?"

Apart from this, they are always very sure of themselves when it comes to theological matters. Notwithstanding their obvious innocence, the perspicacity in their remarks is astounding.

(On my second trip, when Conchita gave me in writing the messages that the Virgin had given her for me, I was overcome by what I was reading, and told her I did not deserve such generosity because I was not good enough and did not make sufficient sacrifices, and Conchita answered with a firmness that is uncommon in an ignorant, uneducated child. "It's enough to do our duty; Our Lady asks no more!")

That night, Conchita gave free reign to her tongue. Between them, she and Aniceta, her mother, recounted with a great sense of humor all the past events: the vision of St. Michael the Archangel; the colloquies they had had with the late Fr. Andreu; Conchita's trip to Santander and the story of her visit to the hairdresser's, where they cut off her plaits. Bit by bit, the house began to fill up. The blazing kitchen fire was too much for me and the air was becoming unbearable.

I was out of the room when Conchita fell to her knees in an ecstasy, and unable to see exactly what occurred.

After kneeling down, she arched over backwards until she was reclining on the floor. All at once, it was as if she was lifted upwards. People round her claimed that not a single part of her was touching the floor, but I cannot testify to this case of levitation because, from where I stood, I could not be certain. When she went out, however, I was able to see what happened to a newcomer to Garabandal, *Señor* Mandoli.

Although a practicing Catholic, he did not believe in visions. I suddenly saw Conchita turn in mid-stride and come straight towards us (*Señor* Mandoli was beside me) to offer him the crucifix. But, either out of shyness, or perhaps to put her to the test, he evaded her. Her head flung back, never once looking to see where she was stepping, Conchita pursued him relentlessly until she managed to get him to kiss the crucifix.

Much moved, *Señor* Mandoli confessed to me that he had just asked the Blessed Virgin, if all this business was true, to make Conchita seek him out and give him her crucifix to kiss.

If my memory serves me right, I was not given the crucifix to kiss that night either. If I did manage to kiss it at any particular point, it was purely by chance in passing as it was offered to someone else.

Walking on, Conchita joined the other three children, who were likewise in a trance. Light of step as usual, they linked arms as they proceeded up the street followed by the crowd.

I recalled that the other apparitions (Lourdes and Fatima) had been local and ecstatic, and it struck me that the ones I was witnessing could perhaps be explained by the ways of our modern times. It was as though the Virgin Mary, like Pope John XXIII, wished to adapt her mercy to the restless

114

seeking of those in need of it.

When you come to think of it, it would look somewhat out of place in these days to see ecstatic trances of the same ilk as those at Fatima and Lourdes. People need another kind of tonic, other methods, another approach. And the methods in the case of these children were perfectly suited to our needs. The apparitions had become "approachable"; everybody could take part in them at a distance; anybody who wished could participate indirectly in the conversations between the visionaries and the apparition. According to the children, from the very first, the Blessed Virgin showed every sign of "desiring to close the gap" between herself and the onlookers. She allowed them to ask her questions; she suggested they give her pebbles to kiss. Altogether, the impression was that she wanted to break down all barriers.

At that moment, however, I was so depressed by the apparent "disdain" that the Apparition was showing me that, without stopping to think of the undoubted generosity she was showing the others, I firmly resolved not to ask any more questions or to expect the slightest sign through the children.

Following a long-standing local custom, in the early hours of Easter Sunday, the village women started to sing the rosary. Despite my weariness, I felt impelled to join them. The devoutness of that scene was truly impressive; I cannot remember ever having spent an Easter of such profound religious fervor as that one.

As we advanced, the night sky cleared. The rooftops shone almost as brightly as the moon and stars.

We must have been mid-way through the third mystery when the unexpected happened.

All at once, I felt someone prodding me in the back. Turning, I saw the Marquesa de Santa Maria arm in arm with Mary Loli. "Mary Loli says she has something to say to you," she confided.

At that moment, I could not think what she was referring to. I remembered that, following her ecstasy that evening (before midnight Mass, of course), I had spoken to the child and she had been as secretive as ever. Just as I had resolved, I had asked her no further questions, and she, for her part, had shown no signs of wishing to talk either. So, I could not grasp what she could possibly want to tell me.

But Rosario Santa Maria added: "It's something to do with what the Virgin told her yesterday, but it seems she was commanded to keep it quiet until after one o'clock today . . ."

Rather abashed, Mary Loli was saying: "Later on; I'll tell her afterwards . . ." We were walking along in procession reciting the rosary, and it was hardly proper to halt for a mere message.

Confused, I did not know whose side to take. But Rosario, who had seen the time I had been having, insisted: "Not on your life; you're to tell her this minute. You can't leave this poor lady with such a worry on her mind."

Mary Loli and I drew slightly away from the procession. Disconcerted, and still fearful of what might be in store for me, I bent down for the little girl to whisper in my ear.

In a clear voice she gave me the message. *"Our Lady says your son is in Heaven."*

I cannot say precisely what happened after that. Everything about me seemed in such a whirl that it is no easy matter to reconstruct the scene. Everything, absolutely everything, was as nought beside that one sentence.

The only thing I remember clearly was hugging Mary Loli as if I were embracing Miguel. Then, I found myself hugging Rosario. She, too, was crying. She was saying so many things at the same time that I could not hear her. People were milling round about us; it was like being on a roller-coaster with more and more people joining us as we spun round. I could see Fr. Marichalar, Fr. Corta, Eduardo Santa Maria, the sergeant-major of the Civil Guard . . . They were all looking at me, fright mingling with emotion in their faces. Alarmed at this interruption, Conchita's mother came over to comfort me. "If she's crying because they haven't given her the crucifix to kiss, tell the lady that they haven't given it to me tonight, either."

They told her mine were tears of joy; the good woman looked relieved. The rest of that rosary was like winging up to Heaven. All my earlier depression had disappeared; I recollect handing Rosario Santa Maria my walking-stick and clinging to Mary Loli's arm. Never in my life had I felt so light-hearted or so secure. Tears still stinging my eyes, we rejoined the procession through the streets in those early hours before dawn. I think I prayed more with my eyes than with my lips. Mary Loli was saying over and over: "Don't cry, don't cry . . ." But, there was no taking any notice of her plea. There was so much to cry about! She insisted: "You ought to be very happy."

Now, I did not bother to look where I was going. I no longer needed a torch; Mary Loli's arm was firm in mine. Full of confidence in her guidance and trust in the Blessed Virgin, I walked the rest of the way gazing up at the heavens. I have never seen the sky so clear and studded with stars; every twinkle was a smile.

It was 3 a.m. when we reached the tavern. Mary Loli's visions had been announced for 4:30 a.m. Still stunned by what had happened to me, I saw Rosario whispering to Mary Loli. "But, my dear child," she exclaimed, "don't keep it to yourself . . .! Tell her now." Coming over to me,

Rosario added: "Mary Loli says the message she gave you is incomplete, but as you started to cry she couldn't go on telling you the rest of it."

What the child had to tell me this time left me still more overcome. "She also told me that your son is very happy, extremely happy, and he's at your side *'every day'*."

She at once went on to confirm what Rosario had already intimated. "I already knew your son was in Heaven; Our Lady told me so yesterday. But she also said, *"Don't tell the lady until tomorrow, after Sunday Mass,' That's why I kept quiet about it until now."*

Such subtlety could not be the work of a child. Moved, I enjoined Mary Loli time and again to tell the Virgin, when next she saw her, to ask anything she wished of me, for, whatever it was, I would gladly give it to her. Afterwards, however, whenever I inquired whether she had conveyed my request to the Virgin, she replied that she had "forgotten." I told myself, by this "forgetfulness," she wished to give me to understand that when the Virgin gave something, she gave it unconditionally.

From the moment of that crisis, everything changed for me. No sooner had the child fallen to her knees in a trance that I had proof that my earlier "ostracism" had ended. She came straight to me. She held the crucifix to my lips once, twice, thrice . . .; then, making the Sign" of the Cross over my forehead, lips and heart, she held the crucifix up for the Virgin to kiss once more and, as if in final confirmation of all she had just told me, she held it out to me again.

Thereupon, without proffering it to anyone else, she went out into the night.

Outside, Mary Loli's father, Ceferino, beckoned us over. "She's talking to the Virgin about you," he said. Sure enough, she was undoubtedly speaking about me. "I told her not to cry, and that she ought to be happy, but she took no notice . . ." After a brief pause, she asked: "And what if she starts crying again when I tell her?"

From that night onwards, they never failed to proffer me the crucifix.

As soon as she emerged from her trance, Mary Loli came over and informed me in a low voice that Our Lady had given her another message. She waited until we were alone. "While I was speaking to the Virgin," she began, "I noticed she was laughing a lot and looking upwards; and, when I asked her why she was laughing so, she replied that, at the very moment she was talking to me, 'he' was looking at you and was very happy ..."

"Who do you mean, Mary Loli? M ..... .?" I could not get his name out.

But she forestalled me. "That's right, Miguel. She said to me: *'Above all, tell the lady that this very minute while I am speaking to you, Miguel is watching her, and that he is full of joy, that he is very happy; very, very happy . . . indeed."*

"Tell me, Mary Loli. How do you know his name is Miguel?"

The little girl was quite unperturbed. Very simply, she replied: "Because I asked her: 'Who is Miguel?' And she said to me: *'That lady's son'."*

I have confirmation of all this recorded on tape. The following day, I begged Mary Loli to record that passage so my husband could hear it. Naturally, the flow of our conversation was less spontaneous than the previous night, but the general lines and atmosphere of it were the same. The little girl seemed bashful about speaking into a microphone. Nevertheless, on my second trip, when she recounted what had happened for my daughter's benefit, in spite of the time that had elapsed, she told the whole story without omitting the minutest detail.

Unfortunately, when he heard the tape, my husband seemed not to be convinced. He had to go to Garabandal before he would admit that what Mary Loli claimed might be true.

Conchita was the last to have an ecstasy that night. It lasted almost two hours. Dawn had already broken when she came to. She was surprised; she fondly imagined only a "short moment" had passed.

I returned to the house where I was lodging, as if I was walking on air. The village was tinged with blue under a sky in which the stars still shone. The first rays of the rising sun were peeping over the mountains.

"She held the crucifix up for the Virgin to kiss. . ."

118

Chapter Nine

THE MESSAGE

The Message of October 18, 1961 signed by the four little visionaries

"We must make many sacrifices, do much penance We must visit the Blessed Sacrament frequently; but first, we must be good and unless we do this, a punishment will befall us.

The Cup is already filling and unless we change, a very great punishment will befall us." The Virgin wants us to do this, so that God will not punish us."

October 18, 1961: an expectant crowd gathers and waits in the rain for the Message to be read

56.—Conchita announced that the Virgin had given them a message. At the express command of Our Blessed Lady, they would make this message known on October 18th (1961).

The news spread all over Spain. On the day, pilgrims arrived in the hundreds, prepared to hear a sensational revelation. Most expected a spectacular miracle. Some even hoped to see the Blessed Virgin. As at Fatima on the day of the miracle of the sun, there was a downpour. Drenched to the skin and up to their eyes in mud, the public waited patiently. The visionaries had been instructed to read the message in church. Some members of the Commission intervened, however, and it was decided to make the announcement up in the pine grove, at 10 p.m. Submissive and obedient, but soaking wet, a very large crowd trudged their way up the steep mountainside at the appointed hour.

In the dim light of a torch, one of the little girls drew from her pocket a piece of paper signed by all four of them. In a weak voice, she proceeded to read the document. She could not make her reedy voice heard clearly, and the message was re-read afterwards by one of the people present. There was nothing very extraordinary about it, nothing spectacular. No miracle was forthcoming. The works of God are always simple, and sometimes even elementary.

The exact text drawn up by the children was couched in the following terms: "People must make many sacrifices and do much penance, and we must pay many visits to the Blessed Sacrament. But, first of all, we must be very good.

120

And if we do not do this, a very great punishment will befall us. The cup is already filling up, and if we do not change, a punishment will come."

At the foot of this message were the signatures of the four children, with their respective ages beside their names.

People's disappointment was quite understandable. Many had been without sleep since the previous day. They had borne with the rain. They had built their dreams around this day, and now, when the time came, all they found was a grubby, crumpled scrap of paper in which four small children asked them to make sacrifices and visit the Blessed Sacrament, all in their atrocious spelling and even worse syntax.

"This is the end of Garabandal," groaned the majority.

Even Fr. Luis Andreu's brother, Fr. Ramon, who had been fortunate enough to see so many wonders in the past few months, began to have his doubts. It was all over as far as he was concerned, too. But, then, a very odd thing occurred. Let us hear his own account of it, taken from a report written at the time.

"I stayed up there, on the mountainside, for about an hour, watching torches descending like a nightmare; at length, I wended my way down to the village. I entered a house to keep dry, but I was feeling so discouraged that everything irritated me. I left, and made for another house in the hopes of seeing familiar faces and not feeling so lonely. A few minutes after I arrived, someone came running to look for me, saying that the children wanted to see me urgently. I was conducted to Maria Dolores' house. There, the little girl took me aside and said: "Father, we've been with the Virgin and we cried awfully, because the Virgin told us that when you went up to the pines you were very happy, but when you came down you were very sad and full of doubts. She told Conchita everything you were thinking and the reasons why you doubted. And she told us to tell you this at once, so you'll cheer up and be at ease, because it really is the Virgin who appears to us."

I went round to Conchita's house. Her only greeting on seeing me enter was: "Are you still sad?" She then proceeded to give me a concise yet exact resume of all my inner thought processes and the reasons for my discouragement. "She told me lots of things about you, and charged me not to tell you for the time being," she added. "Was Our Lady sad? I asked. And she responded: "No, she was smiling."

The general disappointment was hardly surprising in the light of a message that clearly told us nothing new, a message, what is more, that was made known at a late hour on a day that ended in an impressive display of lightning, rolling thunder, rain, hail, pitch darkness and cold.

Nevertheless, overlooking the literary efforts of these children, who barely knew how to write, the meaning of the message is truly in keeping with what the world needs today. It speaks of a punishment which has been announced for a long time. And, to avert this, it demands repentance, sacrifices and penance. The message also mentions devotion to the Blessed Sacrament as a means of reparation, and employs an expression whose meaning was unknown to the children, but which happens to be a piece of Marian terminology, used by the Blessed Virgin on another occasion: "The cup is already filling up . . ."

At Fatima, in their early apparitions, the visionaries likewise saw a large cup in the shape of a chalice into which were falling drops

Mystical Communion. The Host is invisible.

122

of blood. This is precisely the same symbolism the children at Garabandal saw enacted in one of their ecstasies. They later drew a sketch of it to give us.

In this case, it turned out that the little girls were unaware of the meaning of the expression, for they asked several people to give them the right explanation of it, next day.

In the vision of the 20th, Jacinta, who was in an ecstasy, was heard to comment: "Nobody believes us any longer, you know . . . So you must do a great big, big miracle so they'll believe again . . ." But, at this request. Our Lady always smiled and simply answered: "They'll believe . . ."

The Miracle of the Holy Communion

57.—"Here are a few lines with the best of the impressions I have received on this, my third trip, although for me personally, as a priest, it has not been a pleasant one at all because I was not allowed to say Mass or receive Holy Communion, a thing that the children likewise complain about, for they have not received the Lord in their clean little hearts for days on end."[†]

The appearance of a new mystical phenomenon was no doubt due to this prudent situation brought about by superior ecclesiastical orders. This was the administration of Holy Communion by the Angel. The phenomenon is not. a new one in itself. On several occasions, the visionaries at Fatima also received Holy Communion administered by "the Angel of Peace," the shining figure who first appeared to the little children and prepared them for the Blessed Virgin's visits. The same prodigy was frequent in the case of Theresa Neumann and other mystics in the past.

The little girls at Garabandal were often seen to fall to their knees in ecstasy, pray, take up the customary attitude for receiving Communion, open their mouths, and swallow something. A priest once remarked to Conchita: "What you say cannot be true, because angels cannot consecrate." Conchita merely shrugged. But, a few days later, she explained: "I asked the Virgin and you're right. She told me the Angel takes the Hosts from the tabernacles on earth . . ."

Doctors have verified the authenticity of the state of ecstasy when the children take up this attitude and they go through the motions of really receiving Communion. One day, on coming to, Conchita remarked that she was hungry. Her mother offered her a sandwich, and, not daring to taste it, the child said: "But, you see, I've still got a taste of the Host in my mouth."

In her diary, Conchita writes that, at first, St. Michael the Archangel

---

[†] From a letter by a priest whose name we consider it discreet to conceal.

used to give them unconsecrated hosts to teach them how to receive Holy Communion devoutly. One day, he told them to fast the following day, and to bring a little girl up to the pines with them. When they arrived at the pines, the Angel appeared to them "with a cup that looked like gold." He indicated that they should prepare to receive Holy Communion, and that the Hosts were consecrated. He made them say the "I confess . . ." and afterwards they made their thanksgiving and said the "Soul of Christ, sanctify me" in Spanish. Conchita ends her description saying: "And then we told people about it, and some of them made fun of us. And when he gave us Holy Communion, he stayed a long time."

Further on, Conchita's diary reads as follows: "Since we insisted so much with the Blessed Virgin and the Angel that they should work a miracle, on June 22nd, when I was about to receive Holy Communion, he said to me: "I am going to work a miracle; not me, God; but through my intercession and yours." And I asked him: "And what's it going to be?" And he said: "When I give you the Sacred Host, people will see It on your tongue." I reflected a bit. Then I said to him: "But, when you give me Holy Communion, the Host can be seen on my tongue anyway!" And he told me this was not so, that the people round about could not see It. But, the day he performed the miracle. It would, be seen. And I said to him: "But, that is only a little miracle." And he laughed . . . And that day, after telling me this, he went away."

Next day, she again received Communion from the hands of the Angel, and asked him when the miracle would take place. The Angel replied that the Blessed Virgin would tell her the date. When she asked the Virgin the same question, Conchita recounts in her diary that Our Lady revealed that the following Friday she would hear a voice, and the voice would tell her the date.

Her diary goes on: "Friday came, and as the Virgin had told me, while I was in the pines I noticed a voice telling me that July 18th was the day when the miracle would be performed. The voice I heard said to me: 'the little miracle, as you call it'."

In obedience to the instructions she had been given, from July 3rd onwards, Conchita commenced to announce the prodigy of the visible Communion with the same calm and self-assurance that she now shows in foretelling the great miracle which is to come "so everyone will believe."

She wrote the Bishop a letter which was delivered to him personally by Don Placido Ruiloba Arias of Santander, who has seen a great many of the wonders at Garabandal and has shown the utmost prudence and insight in the close check he has kept on the events we are relating.

Hearing that the child was sending letters all over the country announcing the phenomenon, Fr. Marichalar thought it advisable to suggest that she should not write any more. Similar suggestions were put forward by other people, fearful lest the miracle might not materialize. But, Conchita assured them that she was writing on the Angel's orders.

The 18th of July (1962) came, and the streets of the hamlet were filled with a growing throng of pilgrims and sight-seers. As the day wore on, the uneasiness increased with the swelling numbers of the visitors. Near Conchita's house, a village dance was under way to the strains of bagpipes and drums. So it came about that, within a very short distance of one another, there were two groups, one dancing, the other saying the rosary. Since many were afraid that there would be no miracle at all if the dancing continued, Don Ignacio Rubio asked Conchita whether it might not be wise to ask them to stop it. To which Conchita replied that, "dancing or no dancing," the miracle would take place, as she puts it in her diary. "And then," she adds, "they didn't bother about the dancing any longer."

"When it began to get dark," Conchita goes on, "people became uneasy because it was getting late for them, but since the Angel and the Virgin had told me that the miracle would come, I was not worried, because neither the Virgin nor the Angel has ever told me anything would happen which didn't happen."

It is truly admirable to see the faith of this girl who has never for a moment doubted the truth of anything that she has heard in her locutions or from the Vision's lips.

Let us continue to quote from her diary:

"When ten o'clock arrived, I had a summons, and another at midnight. Later, at two o'clock, the Angel appeared to me in my room. In the house were my mother Aniceta, my brother Aniceto, my uncle Elias, my cousin Lucia and Maria del Carmen Fontaneda from Aguilar del Campo. The Angel stayed with me for a while and, as on the other days, he said to me: "Say the 'I confess,' and think of Him whom you are about to receive." I did as I was told, and then he gave me Holy Communion. And after he had given me Communion, he told me to say the "Soul of Christ, sanctify me" and make my thanksgiving, and to keep my tongue out until he disappeared and the Virgin came. And that is what I did. When the Virgin came, she told me that not everybody believed yet."

This is Conchita's account. On falling into a rapture, of course, she had no longer had any notion of what she was doing. The fact is that she entered a state of ecstasy and, her head flung back, walked out of her room, down the stairs and out into the street, followed by the crowds who surrounded her and scarcely let her advance as far as a street-corner, so eager were they all to get as close as possible. There, she thudded to her knees in an impressive fall. She next stuck her tongue out, and those about her could see that it was quite bare. But, a split second later, a thickish white Host formed and she kept it there on her tongue in full view for quite some time.

Here is an account of this inexplicable episode, related by Don Alejandro Damians of Barcelona. Providence dictated that he should find himself some eighteen inches in front of Conchita at the moment of the miracle, and he even succeeded in using his movie camera.

His story reads as follows: "At one time or another, I have been called upon to relate my impressions of the phenomenon which I was lucky enough to see in San Sebastian de Garabandal on July 18th, last year.

Depending on my audience, my frame of mind, the presence of people who had heard the story previously, and many other factors, my story was more or less long, and more or less well told.

To avoid any possible variations (rather than contradictions) that might crop up, I thought it would be a sound idea to confine my account to reading a statement that I myself would write calmly, after due close examination of each point. Some people of reliable judgment advised me to do so, and I resolved to waste no time in drawing up this document which may give you a clear idea of the part I played in events at San Sebastian de Garabandal.

My report starts on Monday, July 16, 1962.

I already knew that the first phenomenon at San Sebastian de Garabandal had been foretold for the 18th; at least, it was to be the first public prodigy of importance, because there, like everywhere else, God's wonders never cease in our day to day existence.

I have always considered myself as a man of faith. I have never needed to see miracles in order to convince myself of the truth of my religion. But, the previous March, human curiosity had already taken me on a visit to the little hamlet in the province of Santander. Without being especially impressionable, I must admit that the kindness of the village-folk, the raptures of the children, the atmosphere of the proximity of the supernatural that strikes one as soon as one sets foot in the place, and the strange inward, personal things that I had experienced there, had all made some impact on my senses. Notwithstanding, I felt that was enough experience in this line, and though I quite looked forward to returning to Garabandal, I was rather undecided about taking that particular opportunity.

I confess that I enjoy my creature comforts, and this is perhaps why I was prepared to spend four days' holiday at our house at Premia de Mar, trying my level best to ignore the fact that, on the 18th, there would take place a spectacle which I was hardly likely to have a chance of seeing again anywhere. I tried to make excuses for my indifference, arguing that, if I was fated to go to the village, then God's will would be done without any help from me.

A cousin of mine was eager to go, and I had left the decision to him. We had arranged that, before setting off, he would pass through Premia on the 16th, on his way back from a town up the coast, to confirm whether or not I should join the party. The time we had agreed on was between six and seven o'clock. I waited in vain, until I finally decided to make myself comfortable and have supper. This I did; by then, I was fully resolved not to interrupt my holiday.

Half-way through supper, my cousin turned up to say that family affairs made it impossible for him to go, but that a friend of his was willing to go if he could only find someone to keep him company on the journey.

I turned the invitation down. My excuses for not going waxed more and more plausible; the lateness of the hour; my cousin's backing out; and the idea of making this trip in the company of someone who was almost a stranger at the time. All these were fine pretexts for my remaining at home.

It was at this juncture, in the most natural way, that I became fully aware of the Divine Will, in the shape of pressure brought to bear on me, not just by my wife and cousin, of whom such a reaction was to be expected, but mainly by my son, whose extreme youth hardly seemed to warrant it. Persuasion by my wife, advice from my cousin, and supplications from my son. At last, I gave in.

There ensued a whirlwind of activity.

A telephone call from Premia to my cousin's friend; our rendezvous for 4 a.m.; the drive up to our Barcelona apartment to pack a bag with the bare essentials and leave a note at my office to say I should be away for a few days. Everything was done in a rush; it was a nightmare.

At 4 a.m. sharp, my friend, his brother, my wife and I departed in a Renault Dauphine.

And now comes a point which was perhaps destined to be the most important of all. Before we drove off, my cousin lent me a movie-camera belonging to a friend of his, giving me a few quick instructions on how to use it, since I was totally ignorant of such matters.

I need not go into any details of our journey. Suffice it to say that we did not bother to sleep on the way, and we reached San Sebastian de Garabandal at about 10 p.m. on the 17th.

The little village was packed with strangers. Without any publicity, the news of the first visible proof had spread all over Spain, and a multitude of people from all parts of the country and every walk of life had brought with them an atmosphere of expectation that could be cut with a knife. Among the visitors were several priests, who were chatting with Fr. Valentin Marichalar, parish priest of Cosio. He had come up to San Sebastian because the following day was the feast of the patron saint of the village.

We found accommodation at the home of Encarna, an aunt of one of the visionaries. There, we deposited our scant luggage and immediately went round to Conchita's, for she was the visionary who had announced the miracle.

That night, we saw some trances. They were as wonderful to behold as ever, and made an even greater impact on us since we were waiting for that visible proof of the supernatural.

It seems absurd to speak of 'the next day,' when, in my mind, the 17th and 18th were all one unbroken day; that night, which I found endless, was chased away by a dim, overcast, leaden-gray dawn that was no more than a continuation of the night hours.

Mass that morning was followed by a slight air of bustle as the village made ready for its celebrations. It was barely noticeable in the morning, but the early afternoon brought mounting expectation.

I spent almost the whole day at Conchita's, with my wife, our companion, several priests and one or two other people.

In the course of the day, I had the opportunity of having a long talk with *Fray* Justo, a Franciscan priest with whom I have since kept up correspondence. In a letter to a friend of mine, he stated how incredulous he had become on leaving Garabandal after the prodigy. It was not to be long before he saw the light and changed his earlier attitude. But, that is another story.

Two factors were present on that occasion to cast doubts on whether or not the expected would take place. One was the festive atmosphere in the village, and the other was the presence of priests.

On certain previous occasions when the first of these circumstances had occurred, the children had not fallen into a rapture. As for the presence of priests, it had always resulted in the child receiving Holy Communion in the normal fashion, and never from the Angel.

The atmosphere certainly lent itself to doubt, because, despite these proven facts, the rumor spread among the visitors that Conchita had personally notified some of the priests to come to Garabandal on the 18th, and that, when questioned about it that very day, she had declared that neither the *fiesta* nor the presence of the priests would prevent the prodigy taking place.

At midday, Conchita announced that she was going to have lunch. This convinced us that, if what we were waiting for was the Communion, then we should have to wait at least another three hours for it.

So, amid doubts, confidence, tedium and hope, that day dragged on into night.

The 18th had passed uneventfully. People were discouraged and openly incredulous.

It was almost one o'clock in the morning on the 19th, and some had already begun to make their way home, when the news spread like lightning that, as measured by the sun, the 18th did not really end until 1:25 a.m.

By that time, those of us at Conchita's house knew one thing for sure; Conchita had received her first summons.

Shortly afterwards, we were asked to go outside. I stood in the doorway with a friend of Conchita's family to prevent anyone entering.

From where I was standing, I could see the kitchen and the staircase leading to the upper floor.

Conchita was upstairs, in company with a cousin and an uncle, I think, when she was seized into an ecstasy. The first I knew was when I saw her descend the stairs very fast, wearing that classic expression which softens and embellishes their features.

As she crossed the threshold, the crowd waiting before the house opened just sufficient time to let her pass, and then the multitude was milling round her, like a river that has burst its banks and sweeps away everything in its path. I saw people falling to the ground and trampled by others. As far as I know, nobody was hurt. But the sight of that fantastic mob on the run, shoving and elbowing one another, could not be more terrifying.

I attempted to follow Conchita, but a crowd, fifteen or twenty feet deep separated us. I sometimes caught a' vague glimpse of her. She turned left along the lane formed by the side of her house and a low wall. She turned left again, and there, right in the middle of the alley, which is fairly wide at that spot, she suddenly fell to her knees.

Her fall was so unexpected that the avalanche of people were carried past on either side of her by the weight of their own numbers. I was fortunate in not being carried past with them, and before I knew it, I unexpectedly found myself to her right, with her face a mere eighteen inches from mine. I staunchly withstood the pushing of those behind me, striving with all my might not to be wrenched from my vantage point. I succeeded.

The shoves gradually ceased and relative calm ensued.

Shortly before midnight, the clouds obscuring the sky had slowly drifted away, and the blue mantle of the heavens had become studded with stars shining about the moon.

In their light, and that of an infinite number of torches in the alley, I could see quite plainly that Conchita's mouth was open and her tongue out in the position customary when going to Communion. She was prettier than ever. Far from causing laughter or looking the slightest bit ridiculous, her expression and attitude had about them an awesome, moving mysticism.

Suddenly, without my knowing quite how, without really realizing it, without Conchita changing her expression in the slightest, the Sacred Host appeared on her tongue. It was totally unexpected. It did not seem to have been deposited there, but might be described rather as having materialized there, faster than the human eye could see.

It is impossible to describe the feeling that came over me at that moment. I still relive it today when I recall it. In these or similar words, I have related the occurrence a thousand times just as it happened, and I have never been able to reach this point without experiencing again those marvelous feelings of tenderness, of love and of joy that bring irrepressible tears to my eyes.

Afterwards, I was told that Conchita had held the Sacred Host motionless on her tongue for about two minutes, before consuming it normally and finally kissing the crucifix in her hand. I was told some months later that this long wait was due to the fact that the Angel had instructed Conchita to keep it in sight until the Blessed Virgin appeared to her.

Personally, I hardly noticed the passage of time. I only remember, as in a dream, voices crying out to me to get down, and I felt a heavy blow on my head.

Hanging from my wrist was the movie-camera. Paying no attention to the protests from behind me, scarcely remembering my cousin's instructions, I pressed the button and filmed the last few moments of Conchita's Communion.

I had never filmed anything in my life before, and I only knew that I had succeeded in focusing on the subject. But, in view of my total lack of experience, I seriously doubted whether the film would come out.

Still in her rapture, Conchita rose to her feet and disappeared from my view, followed by Garabandal *en masse*.

Afterwards, I heard that the ecstasy had lasted almost an hour.

For my part, I had had enough. I stayed where I was, alone in a corner. Leaning back against the wall, I clung to the movie-camera with my last remaining strength. I do not know how long I stood there. When a calm lassitude had replaced the nervous tension in my limbs, I rambled aimlessly through the village streets. I exchanged impressions with people as I went, and finally made my way back to Conchita's house. She was not in a trance now, and she wrote a little dedicatory note for me on a holy picture.

I said goodbye to her and to Fr. Valentin Marichalar, who had sent for me to ask my address. At about 3:15 a.m., feeling totally exhausted, I set out from San Sebastian de Garabandal bound for Barcelona.

Not for one minute did it cross my mind that the movie-camera could have recorded anything. For one thing, there was my ignorance of how to handle the camera, and, for another, the scant light, because the phenomenon took place in the dim glow cast by flashlights. Nevertheless, I took the film to be developed. And now came another "miracle."

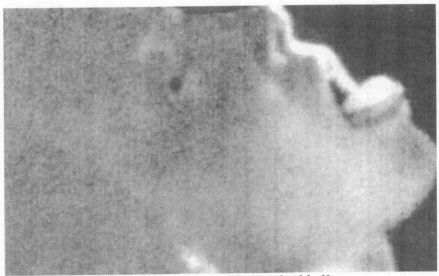

Mr. Damiáns photograph of the Miracle of the Host

"The Sacred Host appeared on her tongue. It was totally unexpected . . . (She) held the Sacred Host motionless on her tongue for about two minutes before consuming it normally . . ."

On the film there appeared seventy-nine frames showing the scene. Jogging by the people around me had resulted in many of the photographs not centering properly on the subject, and they only showed the top of Conchita's head. But, several had recorded the picture quite clearly. Of these, I have chosen one which I enclose with this report.

I do not know what you think of all this, or what decision the Church will adopt after weighing the facts. I honestly have no idea. The only thing I can assure you without the slightest shadow of a doubt is that, on July 18th, 1962, at San Sebastian de Garabandal, two miracles were worked. The first was the Holy Communion administered to Conchita, which was a supernatural occurrence of overwhelming proportions. The second, though just a small miracle, was this sign of the infinite condescension of Our Blessed Lady; for, only her infinite condescension explains my having been there to see the phenomenon in the first place, and its having been recorded on my film."

Conchita writes: "After the miracle which Our Lord God worked through the intercession of the angel, St. Michael, those who had seen the whole miracle, and some of those who had just seen the Host on my tongue, firmly believed; and many of those who had not seen believed it too on hearing the reports of those who had. But, as the days went by, people began to doubt, and some said that it was I who had placed the Host on my tongue. And there was nothing but talk of the Host for a long time."

"A Franciscan Father, Fr. Justo, said it was a lie, and that I was the one who had done it. But, two or three days later, I got a letter from this Father asking forgiveness for thinking so ill of me, and in his letter he said it was the devil who had tempted him. And, shortly after I got the letter, three Fathers arrived, sent by him, because he had to explain many things to them about Garabandal, about the Virgin; and those three Fathers told me that Fr. Justo has spent several very unhappy days and sleepless nights, thinking about the Sacred Host, but that he had now recovered and was very happy and believed very firmly."

Conchita wrote a letter to one of the members of the Commission. In her missive, she complained about his assertion that she herself had been the author of the miracle of the Holy Communion. Here is an extract from that letter: "What a responsibility for me before God! Don't you think I have sense enough by now to think of that . . .? And besides, I would have realized that people would notice; and anyway, I would not be clever enough to do a thing like that. It was the angel, St. Michael, who put a visible Host on my tongue for people to see."

And her letter ends with the following paragraph: "I am also certain the Miracle will come, because the Virgin told me so, and I know the date of the Miracle, too, *and* what will happen in the miracle that the Blessed Virgin is going to work for "the world. I am as certain that the miracle is coming as I am that two and two make four."

Having proved Conchita's genuine state of ecstasy on the day of the visible Communion, it is plain that the unconsciousness, rigidity and other phenomena that occur in a rapture are entirely incompatible with the artificiality of a pretense. The Host seen in the photograph could not have been placed in her mouth by Conchita herself or by any member of the family, because the state of trance makes this deceit impossible.

A Frenchman, whose name we need not mention, was also just in front of Conchita. But, he did not succeed in bringing his movie camera into action. In an interview with *Senor* Damians, both of them witnesses of the phenomenon, he attributed this fact to his not being in a state of Grace at the time. Here is his own explanation of the scene:

"I had everything prepared to film the miracle; everything was ready, but only at the very last moment, in the last fraction of a second, did I get a glimpse of the Host disappearing as the child consumed it. And at that instant, I felt a fearful, horrible pain that overwhelmed me; it was the impression that *I could have glimpsed but He had slipped away from me;* and then, I realized that I was in mortal sin. I felt the need to weep in desperation, and I understood in one instant what Hell must be like, and what it meant to live separated from God. From that time on, I have always lived in a state of Grace, and I hope God will allow me to see the miracle, for I am certain that by doing so I shall recover the inner peace of which I am in need."

◆ ◆ ◆

58.—Let us round off our information on this subject with the evidence given by Benjamin Gomez, a farmer from Potes, who frequently went up to Garabandal and was lucky enough to be in front of the child at the instant she received the visible Communion.

In an interview recorded on a tape recorder, he made the following statement:

"I was little more than a hand's breadth away from Conchita at the moment when she put out her tongue; I saw it was quite bare; there was absolutely nothing on it; I could see her tongue quite plainly, and I assure you it didn't make the slightest motion. All at once I found the Host before me. It was white, shining, It reminded me of the snow when it's iced over and the sun glances off it. But, it didn't dazzle the eyes.

It was the size of a five-*duro* coin,[†] but thicker, as if there were two coins, one on top of the other. It was not quite round. Conchita's face wore that transfigured look this little girl always has in ecstasy. It was the face of an angel. Some people said she must have put the Host there with her hand, or else have had it in her mouth all the time; but I can testify that she didn't move her hands, or raise them to her face either; nor did she draw in her tongue before she stuck it out even farther... It was without moving it that she received the Host... And everybody who was there must have seen this, just as I did, and there were a lot of us. We all had time to contemplate the prodigy at our leisure and without hurry. I didn't believe until that day ... I say that, because it's the truth, and for no other reason, because I'm not so Catholic as to let myself be taken in over this. I have never taken any notice of God in the past, except to curse; or else to offend Him ... I went to Confession last April, but I hadn't been for twenty-three years . . . When I began to come up to Garabandal, the whole village laughed at me. They were surprised that I should be the one to come. 'You've got more sense than to go in for all that', they said to me. And it's true. I have got sense; and that is precisely why I can't help calling a spade a spade . . ."

I have thought it appropriate to include part of his statement in order to show as exactly as possible the evidence given by this tiller of the soil who was a leading witness of the miracle of the Holy Communion in the early hours of July 19th, 1962.

The Miracle Prophesied

59.—The mystery of Garabandal will be cleared up the day of the miracle, the one which Conchita insistently announces and of which she knows many details.

We know that it will come about at 8:30 p.m. on a Thursday coinciding with an event of great importance for Christendom; we also know that it will fall on the feast-day of a saint who is indirectly connected with the Holy Eucharist; and that the miracle will be seen by everybody who comes to Garabandal or its surroundings on that day. What is more, we know that the Pope and Padre Pio will see it from wherever they happen to be; that the sick who are present will be cured, that sinners will be converted, that the miracle will last some fifteen minutes; that the Bishop will raise his prohibition beforehand, so that priests may be there; and that a permanent sign will be left as proof of the miracle, etc.

[†] One *"duro"* is five pesetas. A five-*duro* or twenty-five peseta coin is about the size of a quarter

Just as the punishment we deserve is very great," says Conchita, "the miracle will be as great and spectacular as the world needs." Let us wait trustfully and prepare properly for that great day of the miracle, for it will perhaps be the last chance given us by Heaven, Mary's final effort to make the world leave its road to perdition and, by rectifying in time, ward off its punishment.

If the sun played the main role in the miracle at Fatima, will the moon and the stars be Heaven's messengers at Garabandal?

When the raptures were interrupted, the children kept up their contact with the world of their visions through the phenomenon known as the locution. Says Conchita: "They're like a voice of joy, a voice of happiness, a voice of peace. These locutions have done me a lot of good, because it's as though the Blessed Virgin were inside me. I prefer the locutions to the apparitions, because in the locutions I have her inside me. Jesus will give me the Cross to purify me, and through my crosses He will also make it possible for me to do some good to the world, because without God's help we can do nothing.

So, the locutions confirm the children in their message and in the promise of the great miracle that is coming to make everybody believe. Hence, we can deduce that the hour is near. Let us make ready to know the date of the great prodigy and for God to grant us the grace to be there on the day . . . And let us not fall into the temptation of shrugging our shoulders out of indifference ... If God wants to grant us an exceptional prodigy, we ought to pay attention to Him and show Him due acknowledgement for so great a favor, by preparing to deserve it in the first place, and to show our gratitude and benefit as much as possible from it on a spiritual plane.

To shrug the whole thing off or simply reject it as "unnecessary," as I have often heard devout Catholics describe it, reveals an inner sin of pride that makes us unworthy of such a grace.

Let us live for that day, the day of the confirmation of Garabandal, so that a great many of the Blessed Virgin's children may be there on the day, devout and trusting in her; and so that the message of Garabandal may be spread and obeyed as the works of God so justly require and advise

Garabandal and the nine Pines seen from the south.

"The Miracle will be seen by everybody who comes
to Garabandal or its surroundings on that day."

Chapter Ten

SOME POINTS TO CONSIDER

60.—There is no moral obligation to believe in private revelations. But, this generic affirmation does not mean to say that in certain cases there is not an acquired obligation to believe in them with supernatural faith, on account of the very special attendant circumstances. As the Revd. Fr. John Francis Maxwell says, there have sometimes been facts which have not at first been approved by the Church, and yet God has revealed them to a small minority of people in such clear and conclusive circumstances that these in all conscience prevent them being rejected.

This leads one to the conclusion that, although Christians as a whole are under no obligation at all to believe in the phenomena at Garabandal, which have not for the moment received ecclesiastical approbation, it is none the less true to say that certain people may feel themselves under an obligation to believe them, because Heaven has made them see their reality under conditions that are morally incompatible with doubt.

In this case, the pastoral recommendations should be observed in a spirit of obedience. If the Bishopric recommends priests to abstain from going up to Garabandal, then, those who have obeyed their superiors' orders in exemplary fashion from the very first, regardless of their specific links with these phenomena, are, I think, to be highly commended for their attitude. But, to my mind, this does not mean that those who have been privileged spectators of supernatural happenings should twist their judgement round in order to cease believing in "their truth", the gift so generously given them by God, in the light of which doubts that are perfectly licit and just in another would be morally censurable in their case.

I have a sincere admiration for the approach of those who have managed to fulfill their delicate mission showing both a spirit of obedience and prudent zeal, submitting to ecclesiastical discipline and offering God not only their firm faith in Our Lady of Garabandal, but the sacrifices of their silence, of their renunciation and of the not always pleasant remarks that have been made about them.

May the merits of these anonymous heroes reach Heaven, and serve as a lever to hasten the divine seal of confirmation that we are sure will be forthcoming to clear up this mystery.

The Blessed Virgin in Action

61.—We are living at the height of the era of Marian Apostolate; this is the Marian century referred to by Louis Marie de Montfort when he said that these latter times would be characterized by the Blessed Virgin's presence, which should be understood as a token and promise of the next coming of the Holy Spirit, that is to say, the conversion of the incredulous and the unification of Christians.

The fact is that the Virgin Mary has been appearing to mankind periodically, and her exhortations have been becoming more and more urgent. Similarly, the proof she offers us is becoming more and more spectacular. At Garabandal, a public miracle has been promised. Everything appears to point to the fact that Spain, the altar of Catholicism, has been chosen as the scene for Mary's appeal for the conversion of her children. If mankind does not mend its ways, perhaps the punishment she announces is near. So, the miracle awaited must needs be convincing in order to get through to our reasoning worldly minds. We have already seen that it is to take place at 8:30 p.m., on a Thursday coinciding with an event of the greatest importance to Christendom ... The prodigy will be announced eight days in advance.

Does Conchita know the date . . .? I am inclined to think she does. At least, Circular No. 8 sent out by the Garabandal Information Center, quotes a letter from Conchita which says: "The Virgin will not let me say what the miracle will consist of, although I know this as well as the date, which I can only reveal eight days beforehand."

In her ecstatic colloquy recorded on a tape recorder on the 8th of December, of which I have a copy, she is heard to say to the Virgin, in a breathless, earnest voice as is customary in the visionaries' raptures: "As for the miracle, there's nothing more for me to ask. As I know all about it ... I'm dying for the day to come, so I can tell them . . . People ask me when it's to be ..."

If the issue of Garabandal had not taken the turn it has, with the announcement of a public miracle, this book would in all likelihood not have been written. But the issue is still open and has now reached its most interesting stage: the promise from Heaven has entered a blind alley; either the events at Garabandal are meaningless, or else that little hamlet in the province of Santander is destined to become the final setting for a supreme celestial revolution.

Part Three of the Secret

62.—From all the known private revelations, from the visions at La Salette and at Lourdes, approved by the Church, from the message of Fatima and so on, it can be seen that Our Lady is asking us for prayers, repentance and penance to save mankind from a punishment which will come like the great Flood to restore the balance of Divine Justice.

The secret of Fatima came in three parts. The first part concerned the vision of Hell. The second foretold the 1939-45 World War preceded by a strange light in the sky which was announced by Our Lady. This prophesy was duly communicated by Lucy, and the light was seen without any possible mistake or doubt on the night of January 25th, 1938. The following day, the Press reported the phenomenon. Part three of the message was written out by the visionary and is still sealed in an envelope which was for a long time deposited in the care of the Bishop of Leiria, and is now kept in the Pontifical apartments at the Vatican. This last part of the secret was revealed to Lucy of Fatima by Our Lady as soon as the hair-raising dance of the sun was over.

"You have just seen the prodigy of a short while ago," she said, "the great miracle of the sun. And now, proclaim in my name: A punishment will befall the entire human race. It will not come today or tomorrow, but in the second half of the 20th century. What I revealed at La Salette through the children Melanie and Maximin I repeat today before you. The human race has sinned and trampled with its feet the gift that was bestowed on it. Nowhere does order reign. Satan has reached the very highest places and decides the march of events. He will succeed in introducing himself into and reaching the highest summit of the Church. He will succeed in seducing the minds of great scholars who will invent weapons with which it will be possible to destroy half of mankind in a matter of a few minutes. He will have powerful nations under his empire, and he will lead them to the mass production of these weapons. If mankind does not take steps to stop him, I shall be obliged to let my Son's arm fall. And then, God will punish Man far more severely than when He did so by means of the Flood. The great and powerful will perish in the same way as the weak and small. But a time of severe trials will also come for the Church. Cardinal will oppose cardinal, and bishop will oppose bishop. Fire and smoke will then fall from the heavens, and the waters of the oceans will evaporate; the spray will leap into the sky, and everything that Is standing will sink. Millions of men will perish by the hour, and those who are left alive will envy those who have died ..."

It is better not to go on with the spine-chilling story. Our worries can be summed up in this question: Are these really the contents of the secret that the visionary forbade to be revealed before 1960? Why was the envelope not opened when the date arrived? And, if it was indeed opened, why was the secret not made known?

The document that I have quoted in part above was published on the 15th of October, 1963, in *"Neu-Europa"* of Stuttgart, under the heading "The Future of Mankind". The article was signed by Louis Enrich, and was later reprinted in *"Mensage de Fátima"* of Fundao; *"Agora"* of Lisbon; *"El Pueblo"* of Madrid; *"La Voz de España"* of San Sebastian, etc. The publication of this document was justified by the claim that it was the contents of the secret of Fátima, and that it had been sent by Pope Paul VI to President Kennedy, Mr. MacMillan and Khruschev prior to the Moscow meetings which resulted in the agreement of August 6th, 1963, on the control of atomic tests. The article likewise claimed that the success of the agreement, which has now been signed by ninety countries, was largely due to the influence of this document. *The surprising part is that this news was not subsequently denied by the Vatican as happens whenever something is affirmed as a fact when it is really doubtful;* whence we can reach the terrible conclusion that the news item in question was true.

To ascertain the authenticity of the text, the magazine "Miriam" wrote to the Carmelite Convent at Coimbra, requesting confirmation or denial of the version published. A similar request was sent to the Bishop of Leiria, the diocese to which the Fátima shrine belongs. "We know nothing about the matter," came the reply from Coimbra. On the other hand, the Bishopric of Leiria remained silent.

According to the January-February 1965 number of "Miriam", the most varied constructions may be put on the evasive reply from Coimbra and the dead silence from Leiria. For his part, the Archbishop of Oviedo made a statement to the Press, saying that he "supposed the Portuguese Episcopacy would issue a statement on the subject." But, no statement at all was forthcoming from the Portuguese ecclesiastical, authorities or, for that matter, from the Vatican. This alarming silence, quite contrary to the traditional course taken by the Church, was universally interpreted as meaning that the document of which we have quoted a small part is unfortunately only too genuine. If this is so, then the Treaty of Moscow was not the result of the activity of politicians, but the fruit of Pope Paul's exquisite tact and Vatican diplomacy. And it means that the present generation is gaily, yet unconsciously, sitting on top of a volcano.

There have also been hints that this is not the true original text, but merely the one circulated in diplomatic circles following Pope Paul's appeal to world political leaders. The original text is written in far more hair-raising terms.

There is very explicit proof of the veracity of this document. This is the visit paid to Lucy, on November 26th, 1957, by Fr. Agustin Fuentes, Postulator in the process of beatification of the Fatima visionaries, Francisco and Jacinta. After due ecclesiastical censorship, the contents of their talks were published, in June 1959, in a magazine called *"Fatima Findings"*, and later in *"In Coure de Maria"* (August-September, 1961.)

From their conversation the following points may be gathered:
1.—Lucy is very upset because mankind has not paid the slightest attention to Our Lady's Message, but has trampled the Grace of Fatima in the dust, bringing upon itself a punishment in which millions of people run the risk of perishing.
2.—This situation will end in a decisive battle between Good and Evil, and in this struggle everybody will be forced to take part either on one side or the other.
3.—Mary will win in the end. But at the price of how many misfortunes? This is the point that it lies in mankind's power to avert, or at least allay.

Fr. Agustin Fuentes quotes Lucy verbatim as follows:
"The Lord will punish the world very soon. The punishment is imminent. Just think. Father, of all the souls that are cast into Hell; and this happens because people do not pray or do penance. This is the reason for the Blessed Virgin's great sorrow. Our Lady has often said to me: 'The punishment is on the point of arriving.' And that 'many nations will vanish from the face of the Earth; Russia will be the scourge chosen by God to punish mankind' if we do not obtain the grace of her conversion by prayer and the Sacraments.' Tell them. Father, about the sorrow of the Hearts of Jesus and Mary at the falls of religious and priestly souls . . . There is still time to check Heaven's punishment. We have two very effective means at our disposal: prayer and penance. Three times Our Lady has told me that we are approaching the latter times ... It is urgent that we should realize the terrible truth. And let us not forget that, since the Blessed Virgin gave such great effectiveness to the Rosary, there is no material, spiritual, national or international problem that cannot be solved by means of the Holy Rosary and by our sacrifices. Reciting it with love and piety will enable us to console Mary and wipe away those loving tears shed by her Immaculate Heart."

Conchita begins the New Year well

63.—On January 1st, 1965, Conchita was discovered in a state of ecstasy in the pine grove by two little shepherds who were descending the mountainside to the village with their flocks. Their names were Joaquin, aged twelve, and Urbano, aged nine. According to reports, the rapture must have lasted two hours. The scene, as related by Conchita, is charming. She recalls that she was about to return home after saying her prayers in the pine grove, accompanied by her little dog, when, without warning, she found herself in the presence of the Virgin. "I was overcome with surprise, and knelt there looking at her, and she said to me:

'Hello, Conchita. Where are you off to . . .?'

And I answered her: 'I'm going back to our home . . .'

And that is how the conversation started.

According to absolutely reliable sources. Our Lady of Mount Carmel spoke to her at length. Conchita declares that the Blessed Virgin told her she would give her a fresh message, because people had paid no attention at all to the one made known on October 18th, 1961. The message she is to give will be the last one. "Our Lady revealed to me what the punishment will consist of. But I can't say what it is, except this: it will be an effect of God's Divine intervention, which makes it more fearful than anything imaginable. It will be less terrible for little children to die a natural death than to die of the punishment."

"The punishment, if it comes," she adds, "will take place after the miracle."

However, let us trust in Our Blessed Lady, who is still striving to save us and is offering us now prodigies to overcome mankind's wavering faith, without forgetting her promise at Fatima, where she said: "But, in the end, My Immaculate Heart will triumph."

The document which we have quoted here, and which reveals what is assumed to be Lucy's secret, also ends with comforting promises. "Afterwards, when those who survive all are still alive, the new Kingdom of God will be proclaimed, and Mankind will serve Him once again as in the days before the perversion of the world. Rally all the sincere disciples of My Son Jesus Christ, all the true Christians of these latter times . . .! What a misfortune if this conversion does not come, and if everything remains as it has been until now or in a situation of even graver responsibility! Go, my child, and proclaim this. For this purpose I shall be at your side and shall always be your aid."

We trust that, through her spectacular apostolate, the Virgin Mary will bring about the conversion of Mankind, thus saving it from the collective suicide that threatens it.

Let us beg the Lord for saintly priests

64.—The concern shown by the Blessed Virgin for priests is most striking. It appeared for the first time in her vision at La Salette, and later at Fatima. "Cardinals will oppose cardinals, and bishops will oppose bishops." the document reads. This overt worry, which has also been apparent in the visionaries' talks with Our Lady at Garabandal, calls to mind the persistent recent reports of certain maneuvres of atheistic communism in the seminaries.

On April 13th, 1965, the Madrid daily, "A.B.C.", published an article on this thorny subject. The article in question was called "Los Nuevos Curas," or "The New Priests." On April 24th, the same newspaper published a reply to that article from Don Fernando de Urbina, Director of the Hispano-American Theological Seminary.

If these rumors are true, we need not be surprised if the Church does pass through that phase of opposition and strife between cardinals and bishops, with the implicit risk of internal decomposition which may, through scandal, cause confusion among the faithful.

The arguments of Garabandal's detractors

65.—Some consider it rather undignified, if not somewhat ridiculous, for the Blessed Virgin to appear and spend her time kissing pebbles, medals, crucifixes and wedding-rings.

On the whole, God's works are so simple and elementary that they have at all periods in history seemed ridiculous from a merely human point of view. In the Gospels, we read that, to cure a blindman, Jesus took dust and saliva; today, this would also seem rather ridiculous and not a little odd. That the Virgin Mary should appear so frequently in the early hours of the morning to talk to a few ignorant little girls about matters that often prove essentially to be commonplace is something that the thinking man certainly considers impossible, if he insists that a Heavenly visit should be surrounded by the strict protocol imposed by most of our authorities on earth. But, the Kingdom of God belongs to the little ones, and to see and believe we must become as humble and simple as children. All the visions that have in the long run been granted Church approval have occurred in the midst of details that mankind has in many cases considered commonplace, and in other cases, frankly ridiculous.

Yet, to me, this is further proof of their reality. Indeed, it would be far more alarming if the phenomena had occurred in line with the protocol-laden ideas that modern man has about the proper way to receive a V.I.P.

What is more, does the unusual not serve as a sieve to select, according to their degree of faith, the group of witnesses and followers? Let us not forget that being witnesses of a miracle is a Grace or favor that must be deserved.

When Fr. Valentin Marichalar was replaced as parish priest at Cosio, the Chancery sent a young priest with instructions to be over-prudent, an attitude that required a certain predisposition against the supernatural character of these events.

The fact is, some maintain that, in a place where apparently miraculous phenomena occur, the ecclesiastical authorities should at first be reluctant to believe in the extraordinary. Hence, an essentially prudent approach is adopted, and I do not feel that this attitude can be the object of criticism. The new parish priest was Fr. Amador Fernandez Gonzalez, a good psychologist. He played his part as the devil's advocate to perfection. Determined to accomplish his task as best he could, he kept a close watch on the children at all times. From the first, he declared that the four girls were not putting over a farce or acting in bad faith, but were suffering from an illness that proved difficult to diagnose. Asked whether the Church would accept the authenticity of the apparitions if an unquestionable, proven miracle were to take place, he did not hesitate to say that the Church would not; because the miracle—so he said—would not prove anything either. "It would be a reward from God for the faith of those who asked for it." Perhaps this is twisting matters round to an extreme and making any reasonable solution impossible. But, it is not for us to judge. The Church has her own doctors. Let us simply say that the four children could not perpetrate a fraud for so many months at a time; that, if the visionaries were suffering from some illness, it would have natural effects, and the intensity and frequency of the raptures would long since have ruined their health; that phenomena which arouse in this way religious fervor, the spirit of faith, and love of God and the Blessed Virgin, cannot possibly proceed from extra-natural sources under the influence of the devil. Hence, it seems likely that there are sound grounds for believing that the cause is neither natural nor preternatural, but shows signs of being supernatural.

It should not be forgotten that, throughout the Gospels and the history of the Church, one great fact is evident; as a rule, the works of God, however great they may be, require the cooperation of his creatures.

The peace of mind felt at Garabandal, the spirit of friendship and joy that exists among the "Garabandalistas" or Garabandalites[†] together with everything that has happened there, these are intuitive arguments that lead to an inner conviction tending to belief in the supernatural origins of the phenomena.

What is necessary now is that this faith should grow and spread. But the results may depend on our own behavior. We have received as a gift, an invitation to believe in Garabandal. Perhaps it depends on us whether or not that faith increases, and whether or not the miracle takes place to confirm the supernatural truth of the message; this is the human factor of cooperation which is always required in God's work.[††]

The girls follow their Vision to the door of the church

[†] In her reports. Miss Carmen Cavestany, one of the main witnesses of a great majority of the events at Garabandal, and an unflagging apostle of the Message given out by the visionaries, remarks on the spirit of unity, friendship and inner joy that links all those who saw the unforgettable days of the raptures together. Hers are the following words, taken from her writings on the subject: "Everything at Garabandal leads us to purify ourselves, there and elsewhere, by living the Message in our daily lives." "Conchita wrote me saying that the Blessed Virgin wants the Message to be spread throughout the world." "We should form a sort of union of all of us who go to Garabandal, committing ourselves to a common programme, namely, fulfillment of the Marian Message."

[††] This chapter had already been written when news was received that Conchita had had the announcement of what she calls a "warning so that the world will make amends". "This warning," she says, "is like a punishment, for the just and the wicked alike; for the just, so as to bring them closer to God, and for the wicked to announce to them that time is running out, and that these are the last warnings. It is very long; I cannot explain it by letter. Nobody can prevent this coming. It is a certainty, although I do not know the day or anything about the date." From this paragraph, taken from a letter written by Conchita, it can be deduced that the punishment will, or will not, come, depending on the conduct of the human race. But, what is certain is that, before the possible punishment, and as a last means of persuasion to convert mankind, there will be an appeal from Heaven that will cause a state of tension and great fear.

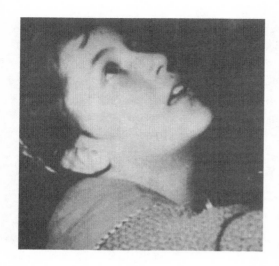

Mary-Loli in ecstasy

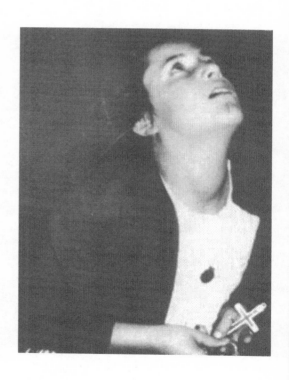

"In their trances, the children's faces underwent a complete change, turning radiant and softly beautiful."

Chapter Eleven

THE CHANCERY OF SANTANDER

66.—On September 7th, 1961, the Press[†] published the following statement issued by the Bishopric of Santander concerning the "Apparitions at San Sebastian de Garabandal".

"In the light of the constant questions put to Us with regard to the nature of the events taking place in the village of San Sebastian de Garabandal, and in our desire to guide the faithful in the correct interpretation of the same, we have felt obliged to study them thoroughly for the purpose of fulfilling our pastoral duty.

To this end, We appointed a commission of persons of well-known prudence and doctrine to inform us about the said events objectively, competently and with every guarantee.

In view of the report that has been submitted to Us, we believe it is too early to give any final judgment concerning the nature of the phenomena in question. Nothing so far obliges Us to affirm the supernatural origin of the events that have occurred there.

In the light of this, and final judgment remaining subject to the events that may take place in the future. We hereby declare that:

1. It is our desire that priests, be they of this or any other diocese, and members of the clergy of both sexes, even independent clergy, should for the time being abstain from going to San Sebastian de Garabandal.

2. Until such time as the ecclesiastical authorities pass final judgment on this matter, We advise the faithful to try not to go to the said village.

By these provisional steps, We certainly do not obstruct Divine action on souls; on the contrary, once the spectacular nature of the events has been eliminated, the light of truth will be greatly assisted."

Shortly afterwards on October 27th of the same year, the Bishopric of Santander published a fresh communique which read as follows:

"Respecting the events that have been taking place at San Sebastian de Garabandal, a village within our Diocese, We are bound to tell you that, in fulfillment of our pastoral duty, and to forestall any hasty or imprudent interpretations by those who venture to pass final judgment where the Church does not yet consider it wise to do so, as also to serve as guidance for souls, We have decided to make the following statement:

[†] Quoted from the Madrid daily, "YA".

1. There is no proof that the said apparitions, visions, locutions or revelations can so far be presented as true and authentic, or be held as such on any serious grounds.

2. Priests should refrain absolutely from anything that might contribute to creating confusion among the faithful. Let them therefore carefully avoid, as far as they are concerned, the organization of visits and pilgrimages to the said places.

3. Let them soberly and charitably enlighten the faithful as to the true attitude of the Church in these matters. Let them make them understand that our Faith does not need the support of as yet unproved revelations and miracles to maintain it. We believe what God has revealed and the Church teaches us; the clear, genuine miracles of Jesus Christ fall within this category. He gave them to us as proof of his doctrine, to which there is nothing to be added. If He, Himself or through His Blessed Mother, thinks fit to speak to us, we should be attentive to hear his words and say to Him, like Samuel: "Speak on, Lord, Thy servant is listening."

4. Let them likewise teach their parishioners that the best preparation to hear the voice of God is perfect, whole-hearted humble submission to the teachings of the Church, and that nobody can benefit from hearing the voice of Our Father Who is in Heaven, if he proudly rejects the doctrine of our Mother the Church, who welcomes and sanctifies us on earth.

5. As for you, beloved faithful, do not let yourselves be seduced by any doctrine that comes along. Harken calmly and trustingly to the teachings of your priests, placed at your side to be the Church's true teachers.

I know that you have felt impatient and expectant, and that many of your minds became perturbed at the approach of these recent days. I should like to bring to your minds the peace and tranquility which is the basic prerequisite for serene, balanced judgment. Let nobody snatch from you the precious gift of that peace which lies in God, and as St. Paul says to the Thessalonians: "do not be thrown into confusion, by any spiritual utterance, any message or letter . . ."

It can be seen from these statements that, in view of the numbers of people who were flocking from all over the country, and the repercussions that these events were having inside and outside Spain, the Chancery deemed it wise to relieve the tension, which is not appropriate in cases of phenomena of this kind.

In doing so, the Chancery simply gave further proof of its proverbial foresight. But, having read both documents thoroughly, there is nothing to indicate that the events at Garabandal are denied, or condemned by the Church, as some people make out.

In the first note, the Chancery's reasoning is summed up in the following words: *"In view of the report that has been submitted to Us, We believe it is too early to give any final judgment concerning the nature of the phenomena in question."*

After saying that *"nothing so far obliges Us to affirm the supernatural origin of the events,"* it ends by declaring, *"final judgment remaining subject to the events that may take place in the future."*

The second note was produced after the groundless disappointment caused among those present by the message of October 18th, because most people who went to the village were convinced that a spectacular miracle would take place at that moment. This note does not deny the phenomena either, but simply says that "there is no proof that the said apparitions, visions, locutions or revelations can *so far* be presented as true and authentic, or be held as such on any serious grounds." Hence, it does not discard the possibility that they may prove to be authentic later on. It simply recommends calm and serenity in view of the fact that many people had become perturbed about the events that were awaited.

We most sincerely acclaim the prudent approach adopted by the Church, setting people's minds at rest and recommending them to wait; this does not mean to say that some of their informants may not have adopted personal attitudes with injudicious results, because an excess of zeal can be as harmful as a lack of it. But, quite understandably, even if a conductor leads his orchestra well, when it is formed of many musicians with different repertoires and abilities, it is no easy matter to prevent one or two playing a note or two off key . . .[†]

[†] When His Excellency, Bishop Eugenio Beitia Aldazabal took possession of the Diocese of Santander, he published in the "Boletín Oficial del Obispado" (Official Gazette of the Bishopric) a decree dated October 7th, 1962, in which he ratified and confirmed the contents of the notes published by the Apostolic Administrator, the Revd. Doroteo Fernandez Fernandez. This decree begins as follows:

"THE SPECIAL COMMISSION, set up to study the events occurring in the village of San Sebastian de Garabandal, submitted the corresponding report to us on October 4th of the present year. The said COMMISSION maintains its previous position, and finds that those phenomena lack any supernatural origin, and have an explanation of a natural order. In consequence . . . etc., etc."

I have thought fit to quote the heading of the decree so that it may be seen that the "attitude of the Bishopric is perforce a consequence of the reports which it received from the Special Commission in question, to which the Bishop always refers in capital letters; for, with the Commission rests the responsibility for a series of resolutions which we, in principle, consider to have been arrived at hastily, and which are fully justified in light of the findings of the Commission and the proverbial prudence of the Church.

"What is happening at San Sebastian de Garabandal?"

67.—A few months after the last note from the Chancery of Santander, an unsigned article appeared under this title. It think it deserves to be quoted here, for it is a perfect, objective summary of all the events we have covered. It reads as follows:

"For many months now, a great number of people have been asking themselves: 'What is happening at San Sebastian de Garabandal?' "

The four little girls who see the Virgin, and who have had no rest for the last eleven months, make the most amazing statements in all simplicity, and set an example of penance and charity.

Mary Cruz, Jacinta, Maria Dolores and Maria Concepcion claim that they see the Virgin. The children are certainly not lying. If they say that they see the Virgin, then they see her. The questions which we all ask ourselves on arriving at Garabandal are: How and why do they see her? Why don't other children see her? Why, when at certain times they want to see her, do they not succeed in seeing her? Why do all four children see her together? Why do they see her separately? Why are the apparitions announced to them in advance? Why do days at a time go by without any of them seeing her, until the foretold date arrives? Why do such amazing and profoundly sublime things happen here, in such simple surroundings?

Legend and truth have mingled to become almost inseparable one from the other. Rumors, lies, distortions of the truth have been mixed up with the real facts. This is only natural; but to get to know the facts properly, one has to resort to firsthand experience.

The solutions that have been put forward by members of the medical profession have been refuted one after the other, and there always remains an element of doubt about any medical explanation. The four girls are normal; they have been the witnesses of countless extraordinary happenings, and they are not lying. Clairvoyance, metempsychosis, hysteria, suggestion, auto-suggestion and many other words defining pathological and neurotic states, etc., have all in turn been invoked.

Meanwhile, the four girls go on seeing the same personages, hearing them, receiving lessons in obedience and humility; they are docile and humble. The Virgin has invited them to be charitable, to be well-behaved, and to do penance for the sins of mankind.

Both their simplicity and their spirit of penance are astonishing As if it were the most natural thing in the world to do, they have risen at five or six o'clock in the morning throughout the winter to go and say the rosary in the *"cuadro"*, the enclosed spot where the first apparitions took place. After seeing this, one doctor exclaimed: "Hysteria is far more comfort-loving than all this."

It is a fact that they have spoken sentences in English, French, German, Latin and Greek; and the most amazing part of it is that, by repeating what they heard, they gradually corrected themselves until they pronounced the words properly.

I know of several cases of reading of consciences, and all of them have been both accurately and charitably done. The person in question has been the only one to know about it in each case. They have spoken about matters of which they were totally ignorant.

Their insensitiveness to outside pain is complete. They go through the streets at a slow walk, and sometimes they run at an incredible speed. The sharp, painful stones seem to soften beneath their feet.

From the spiritual point of view, conversions to a better way of life have been so many that this hamlet appears to have turned into a source of sanctification. A French Jewess, a Protestant German engineer, and an American engineer, to name but a few, have found the road to Catholicism here.

Crowds have flocked to the scene in countless numbers, like a rosary of wonderment and devotion, to see these children who ought in point of fact to be exhausted or dead by now, but who show every sign of absolute normality. The foreign Press has reported these events in a number of well written articles.

A gentleman who lay in a hospital in Switzerland following a car accident felt Our Lady's call, and made a pilgrimage in thanksgiving for the inward grace received. A lady came all the way from Algeria to ask the Blessed Virgin to protect her son's life. She walked the last four miles barefoot.[†]

Many people have come in thanksgiving for unusual recovery of health and cures. There is talk of instantaneous mending of broken bones in Barcelona; last degree tuberculosis cured in a flash in Cadiz, etc.

It is a fact that great spiritual benefits are received here.
I have spoken to some of the people who were pointed out to me as having actually received these graces. I know that they have had to suffer because of it, but I also found that they are the most amazed of all at the things they have seen.

How is it that the four girls at Garabandal have managed to prophesy events that have subsequently occurred at the time foretold?

[†] The sacrifice of walking barefoot up the steep rough track from Cosio to Garabandal has been made by many people, including two ladies of leading Santander families, who, despite their pregnancy, did not hesitate to offer the Blessed Virgin this fearful penance.

How is it that everything is so confined to the spiritual plane? Why are doctors, industrialists, theologians, educated people and simple people alike, all baffled by what they see?

This is but a small fragment of the ensemble of prodigious happenings that draw people in their thousands to the picturesque rural scene.

There are four girls, and in a few days' time a year will have passed since their first apparition. At 10 p.m. on August 8, these children saw how the Blessed Virgin announced his coming death to Fr. Luis Maria Andreu, a Jesuit priest. Fr. Andreu died without any agony at all, passing from his normal state to death instantaneously, after declaring: "Today is the happiest day of my life." He died six hours after his death was announced.

The girls offer their crucifixes to people to kiss, and whether or not they make the Sign of the Cross in blessing, they serve as the vehicle of God's Grace, which touches people's hearts and brings tears to the eyes of the strongest among us.

So great a number of cases are there, that a whole book would be necessary to relate them all.

The only thing one needs when one goes to Garabandal is some spiritual training and good will.

Our Holy Mother the Church, as Mother of us all, will guide us along this pilgrim's way with her boundless prudence. And it falls to her to have the last say in this matter. The Apostolic Chancellor of the diocese of Santander wrote in October 1961, even before the time factor had become yet another argument in favor of these events, among other pastoral advice, "If God, Himself or through His Most Blessed Mother, thinks fit to speak to us, we should be attentive and listen to his words, saying to Him like Samuel: 'Speak, Lord, Thy servant is listening'."

Chapter Twelve

CONCLUSIONS

68.—We have already said that, in all the revelations to mankind, the Divine factor has demanded human cooperation, and our response has always had a great influence on the subsequent course of events.

At Garabandal, the Angel did not appear the day after his first apparition, perhaps because a gang of small boys threw stones at the scene of the prodigy. The miracle of the visible Communion, announced for July 18, took place in the early hours of the 19th, perhaps on account of the dancing which the village youths did not want to forgo. When people came to the village in a spirit of scant devotion or respect, we have seen that the Vision departed, after complaining to the visionaries at this conduct ... In fact, this behavior on the part of the Vision is not only to be found at Garabandal. The same thing occurred at Fatima and all places where phenomena of this kind have taken place. When the little Portuguese visionaries were kidnaped by the Mayor of Ourem and could not keep their appointment with Our Lady on the 13th of the month, the Vision appeared on the 19th instead, and told them that the miracle announced for October would be less spectacular owing to the kidnaping incident. Human conduct has always influenced the Divine attitude, and this is hardly to be wondered at. If the master of the house receives his visitor with bad grace, however kindly the visitor may be, the host will eventually lose his friendship and not see him again. If this behavior is observed in the case of important people, such as a prince or a king, for instance, their absence later is even more justified, because the discourtesy and offence is far worse. And how would one go about describing a reaction of marked discourtesy and outright assault against One who sets aside the physical laws of Nature to come to us in God's name and deliver a message for our salvation? Prudence is no justification for a rude reception. Prudence demands what the Church has done in this case, namely, avoidance of hasty discussion and not granting official approval to events before the prophesies are confirmed and their circumstances fully clarified. But, for a mere investigator or a member of a commission, this attitude of prudence is quite compatible with respect, a private wish to see everything confirmed eventually, love of Our Blessed Lady, and a spirit of faith. Both attitudes are indeed compatible, even though the latter may not be expressed openly. This is particularly so when, from the phenomena themselves, it is clear that there are more than sufficient grounds for a minimum of hope.

To twist things around so as to find a natural explanation for incomprehensible happenings is pointless. Hastily to express negative opinions when highly experienced people are in doubt or assert the contrary is hardly wise. To dismiss the whole thing, just to avoid complications and further bother is not just. The very prudence of the Church requires that her silence should last as long as possible. But, prolonging her silence does not mean to say that she should elude a hasty "yes" by coming out, instead, with a hasty "no". That is why the notes issued by the Bishop leave the issue undecided, and simply state that "nothing so far obliges Us to affirm the supernatural origin of the events, final judgment remaining subject to those that may take place in the future." Hence, the denial of the events did not proceed from the Bishop; this denial and the hurried, unreasonable judgments bandied about proceeded from certain individuals who, emitting their comments, made use of an authority with which they are not in fact vested.

Our Lady of Fatima was displeased at the conduct of the Mayor of Ourem, a freemason, an atheist, and a self-declared enemy of the Church (Heaven subsequently punished him, for he was blown up by a bomb which he himself was carrying in a briefcase, intending to throw it at a political rival passing in a procession). And if this is so, how much greater displeasure Our Lady must feel at similar behavior on the part of people who, being Catholics, are duty-bound to examine the phenomena calmly, showing cautious zeal, great charity, faith and love of God.

We are all undoubtedly bound to make mistakes. To make an error of judgment is innate in our human condition. There is no denying the fact that even heinous crimes have been committed in the name of high ideals. It is a proven fact, admitted by the Church, that, invoking prudence, the Inquisition sentenced holy innocents to death. St. Joan of Arc was dragged to the stake by a group of good men who were scandalized by the things which the young maid heard and said, and it now turns out that what she heard was God, and what she said was holy.

Only the voice of the Church when She makes a solemn statement should be harkened to in a spirit of absolute submission and obedience. Outside Church matters, we live in a perpetual state of improvement and progress, modifying our viewpoints and correcting our errors. Even within the Church, the recent sessions of the Vatican Council have given ample proof that there was much to be rectified, and that all discussion on issues that do not affect dogma is good as long as it is charitable and in good faith.

In saying this, it is my intention to enlighten certain people who consider a person's private opinion as an undoubtable axiom, simply and solely because that person wields a little authority. Their ignorance carries them even farther; it leads them to follow that private criterion unquestioningly, even though their own personal convictions, arrived at in the first place because of what they have seen and heard, cry out to them to do just the contrary. I was deeply impressed by the sincere sorrow of a mother, recounted in a book on Fatima:

"I was unable to see the miracle of the sun, because my confessor forced me to cancel the trip ..."

More than ninety thousand people are estimated to have stayed at home on the day of the miracle, deaf to the Blessed Virgin's appeal, due to others who brought to bear on them powers that lay beyond their real attributes, and forbade them to believe in "visions". But, it afterwards turned out that the vision was true and Our Lady's invitation genuine. So it was that those poor people submitted in blind obedience and missed the *unique* opportunity of their lives. Perhaps some of those souls, whose lives were bound to have changed, had they but seen the miracle, are now deprived of God's presence because they followed that unfortunate piece of advice. What a responsibility for those who were truly to blame!

Therefore, though I admit my own lack of authority in the matter, I venture to advise prudence; prudence of the kind that does not require one to rush into affirming or gainsaying anything too quickly.

True enough, a commission appointed by the Chancery of Santander stated that there is a natural explanation for everything that has happened at Garabandal; a natural explanation—be it said in passing—which neither competent doctors nor specialized theologians have been able to find. But it is no less true that another commission, acting privately with the permission of the same Chancery, came to the opposite conclusion. Which of them was right?

When and if the miracle takes place, it would be most regrettable if many people were to fail to see it, as happened at Fatima, because the guidance given them was inspired with excessive prudence. For the Garabandal case is not over. The day the issue is closed, we shall be the first to accept the decision, be it "yes" or "no", and write as an epilogue to this account the ending which only Heaven can give us.

I should not like what I say to be misconstrued. But, I feel compelled to say it because of the attitude of some Catholics who consider themselves "more Catholic than the Pope". To justify my view, let me relate a short anecdote.

I am friendly with a writer who specializes in Marian subjects. I thought that he might be interested in seeing a filmed report on Garabandal. I have a series of carefully selected slides and a taped commentary to go with them, which includes the recorded voices of the girls saying the rosary while in an ecstasy, and some of their conversations with the Blessed Virgin. I also have a number of films of certain ecstasies. Quite apart from the authenticity of these events, I think all this has a human value for everybody, and especially for someone who is known to be an expert on the subject. The impact of the filmed account is tremendous. It effectively arouses and strengthens ones love of God and of the Blessed Virgin. On the other hand, there is no Church provision forbidding one to look at photographs of Garabandal. Be this as it may, my offer was indignantly turned down, with much touching of wood and astonishment that anyone should have been rash enough to make such a proposal, which he saw as the most heinous of sins. Calling on all my powers of understanding, I respect his opinion, but I must confess that it strikes me as absurd.

Garabandal—I repeat—still remains a mystery. Our Lady, who almost "lived" in the village for most of 1961 and 1962, was absent for a time, it is true . . . Why? Perhaps it is the human element that is to blame, for, in my view, it has failed her rather badly. But, even though she was absent, she did not sever the contact. She is still "carrying on the correspondence" as we might call it, if the expression is not irreverent, and in her "letters" she promises to return on the day of the great miracle.

On December 8, 1964, she "called" Conchita in a locution to greet and congratulate her on her Saint's day.[†] On January 1st, 1965,

---

[†] When Conchita came out of church saying that she had had a locution, a priest who was there at the time asked her to give him a written account of the phenomenon. Then and there, in the sacristy, taking up pen and paper, she spontaneously proceeded to write with the greatest of ease the description given below:

"While I was giving thanks to God and asking Him for things, He answered me. I asked Him to give me a Cross, for I am living without any suffering other than the suffering of not having a Cross to bear, and when 1 was asking this of Him, Jesus replied: *Yes, I shall give you the Cross*: and, much moved, I went on asking Him for more things, and I said to Him: "Why is the miracle coming? To convert people? And He replied: *To convert the whole world.* Will Russia be converted? *She will also be converted and thus everybody will love Our Hearts.* And will the punishment come after that? And He did not answer me. Why have You come to my poor undeserving heart? *I have not come for your sake; I have come' for everybody's sake.* Is the miracle going to happen as if I were the only one to have seen the Blessed Virgin? And He responded: *For your sacrifices, your forbearance, I am allowing you to be the intercessor to work the miracle.* And I said to Him: Would it not be better if it were all of us, or, otherwise, if You did not make any of us the intercessor? And He said to me: *No.* Will I go to Heaven? And He replied to me: *You will love very much and you will pray to Our Hearts.* When will You give me the Cross? And He did not answer me. What will I be? And He did not answer. He only said that *wherever I am and whatever I do, I shall have much to suffer.* And I said to Him: Will I die soon? And He responded: *You will have to be on earth to help the world.* And I said to Him:

156

She announced a new apparition of the Angel for the 18th of June. This announcement was a most important prophesy for the happenings at Garabandal; in the first place, because it was a prophesy made six months in advance. As Dr. J. M. Bonance said at the time: "Let the supporters and opponents of the supernatural origin of Our Lady of Mount Carmel's apparitions take this unprecedented opportunity of confirming their opinion and of correcting it. It is a new invitation open to all mankind, with far longer notice than the famous miracle of the Sacred Host on July 18, 1962."

What is more, this forecast of the date was a sign of the Virgin Mary's benevolence, because, if the prophesy turned out to be true, mankind would be better able to prepare for the announcement of the great miracle, whose authenticity it would then prove difficult to question . . .

Ecstatic walk of Mary-Loli and Jacinta, May 1962.

I am worthless, I shall not be able to help at all. And He said to me: *By your prayers and sufferings you will help the world.* When people go to Heaven, do they go dead? And he said to me: *People never die.* I thought we did not go to Heaven until we were resurrected. I asked Him whether St. Peter was at the gates of Heaven to receive us, and He said: *No.*

When I was in this prayer or conversation with God, I felt outside this world.

Jesus also told me that there are now more people who love His Heart. About priests. He told me 1 must pray hard for them, so that they may be saintly and do their duty and make others better. *That they may make Me known to those who do not know Me; and that they may make Me loved by those who know Me, but do not love Me.*

Mary-Loli and Jacinta follow the Apparition through the village.

"These girls are not lying; they see 'someone' . . .

SUMMARY

69.—To sum up, from everything we have mentioned here, phenomena and other circumstances checked by thousands of eyewitnesses, from the photographs that exist by the hundred; from the tape recordings of the dialogues and prayers in ecstasy; from the films that have been taken; from the tests made to ascertain the veracity of the ecstasies; from the medical inspections and reports; from the state of health of the children, devoid of the slightest pathological symptoms; from the miracle of the Communion announced in advance and photographed; from all the circumstances surrounding the death of Fr. Luis; from the graces obtained through the mediation of Our Lady at Garabandal; from the interrogations and studies undertaken by theologians and experts, etc., one indisputable fact transpires: *these girls are not lying,* these girls see "someone" who speaks to them, corrects them, teaches them, informs them of things of which they are ignorant; announces to them prophesies that are fulfilled; gives them directions in order to find lost objects; permits them to gain knowledge of the state of the consciences of certain people; enables them to identify priests in lay clothes, and to answer questions framed solely in their minds . . . All these are completely verified phenomena, which defy any natural explanation.

We do not know whether the cause is preternatural or supernatural. But, in view of the type of message in question, the conversions that have taken place and the fervor aroused, we cannot help thinking, (prompted by those words spoken by Jesus, "by their fruit thou shalt know them") that the prodigies are due to supernatural causes. It is true that, for the moment, the Church has not seen fit to pass final judgment, but, on the Vision's behalf, the children long since announced this period of contradictions, doubts and misgivings which have in fact made their appearance and which, given the proverbial prudence of the Church, were the reason for the denials in the first place.

But, over and over again, after foretelling this negative phase, the Vision insisted that *the miracle will take place and people will believe.* And everything that this strange Vision has said has hitherto been fulfilled to the letter. It announced the miracle of the Holy Communion, and the miracle was performed; it announced that the children would have much to suffer and would come to doubt everything, and the children did in point of fact have their moment of vacillation, a black night that seemed to engulf their souls.

But, their locutions continue. The raptures are back . . . For on June 18, 1965, a new angelical apparition was announced, and as we have seen, all the circumstances surrounding the miracle are known.

Why should we consider the case closed precisely now, when it has reached its most promising point?

Let us admit the truth. The question mark remains, the investigation is not over. Garabandal is still a mystery which, as Catholics and men of conscience, we are still duty-bound to follow respectfully and zealously. Only in this way, when the miracle is announced, will it find us prepared, thus avoiding the Blessed Virgin's voice being drowned in the silence of surprise or ignorance.

If Mary calls us, an immense multitude should be on hand to obey her summons and witness the gift which she offers us, that marvelous spectacle which will come as a seal to ratify the divine message from Heaven. Will the same happen with us now as happened at Fatima, where twenty-five years had to elapse before the world heard Our Lady's message?

May our sacrifices and our prayers, our conduct, cooperate with Heaven so that the issue of Garabandal may soon be resolved and shown to be an undeniable truth.

And I close these pages, thanking Mary for having granted me the opportunity of seeing, believing and taking up my pen on her behalf, at a time like this when confusion, heated debate, doubt and misgivings reign supreme, and so much has been said and written in favor of and against Garabandal. The circumstances of life are often confusing and mislead one, and the author of this book, who has been fortunate enough to write in defense of the Marian apparitions and messages, could just as easily have fallen into the same temptation as Monroy,[†] whom I sincerely invite to accompany me on the day of the celestial appointment awaited by all. For, I feel sure that, if the miracle takes place and the whole matter is cleared up, he will admit his mistake about Garabandal, as I am prepared to recognize my own possible errors of appreciation, and that he will take up his brilliant pen again, this time to devote to the Blessed Virgin a warm, fervent prayer for forgiveness, showing his indebtedness and his love . . .

---

† See Appendix

THE STORY OF A TRIP

70.—This book had already been printed and only needed binding when June 18, 1965, arrived.[†] This was the date for which Conchita had announced an apparition of St. Michael the Archangel. That date was also the fourth anniversary of his first apparition. Conchita prophesied the ecstasy more than five months in advance. The Blessed Virgin foretold it on New Year's Day. From that time onwards, she did not hesitate to announce the event to all who asked about it.

Accompanied by Fr. Luna, a zealous priest from Saragossa, I arrived at Garabandal at 2 p.m. on June 17th.

The village was packed with cars from many countries. It was no easy matter to find room to park. I abandoned my car in a narrow street which it virtually blocked, thanking my stars that, fortunately in San Sebastian de Garabandal there were no traffic police and, for the time being, no parking rules.

"The village was packed with cars from many countries . . ."

We walked round the streets, greeting acquaintances. We first of all met the Marques and Marquesa de Santa Maria. Not far behind them was Mary Loli. Fr. Luna, who was on his first visit to Garabandal, had a chance to talk to her. We admired her simplicity, her sweetness, her charm, that affable, amazingly natural welcome so characteristic of the four girls.

[†] The author is referring to the first Spanish edition.

We had been chatting with Mary Loli for a while when Mary Cruz came up. They both accompanied us to church. Coming out of the church we saw Jacinta. Fr. Luna spoke to her for a moment, until we left them all besieged by pilgrims. We then made our way to Conchita's house. We had heard she was ill in bed. This piece of news had given rise to very varied comments. Many thought it was an excuse since she had committed herself by announcing the apparition. But the truth of the matter was that Conchita had had a heavy cold for two days, and that very morning she had had a temperature of 101°. She felt better in the afternoon, however, and got up. When we reached her house, she was chatting amicably with a party of visitors, sitting on the bench by the door.

"Do you expect to see the Virgin?" one asked.

"No, not the Virgin; only the Angel," she replied, her manner very natural.

"And what if there's no apparition?"

"The Virgin can't tell a lie."

"Are you sure, then?"

"Of course, I'm quite sure." And she smiled, calm yet gay, puzzled that anyone should have misgivings about the apparition on the following day.

I was taken aback by Conchita's astounding memory on that occasion. The pilgrim with whom she was talking remarked that this was his second visit. Conchita reminded him of the month in which he had come on his first visit, and described the people who had accompanied him, details which the pilgrim himself appeared to have forgotten.

162

June 18, 1965: The crowd gathers and waits for Conchita.

We sat there for a long time, overcome with admiration at the very appropriate replies she had for everybody, ever ready with a joke or some of that innocent fun that always enlivens her conversation.

I remember someone remarking to her that, with so many foreigners arriving, she would have to study languages to understand everybody.

"On the contrary," Conchita replied, "if I don't know the language, it saves me answering things that I shouldn't or that I don't understand."

I hazarded an indiscreet question.

"Do you know roughly what time the apparition will be?"

She looked at me and smiled, but did not answer. I assumed the answer to be in the negative, but the following day I discovered that she had said nothing so as not to tell a lie. The fact was that Conchita knew every circumstance of the ecstasy that had been announced.

We took our leave and continued roaming the village streets, from house to house, from one group to another. At Garabandal one knows everyone, greets everyone. The soul blossoms out and people fully express both their ideas and their feelings. The afternoon sped by. I spent my time chatting with people, getting firsthand accounts of many earlier events in the village. I had a long talk with Fr. Valentin Marichalar, with Don Placido Ruiloba, with the sergeant-major of the Civil Guard who had been stationed in the district when the apparitions were frequent (he had come all the way from Barcelona to see this one), with Don Benjamin Gomez, the witness of the miraculous Communion. I also spoke with

Mercedes Salisachs, Don Maximo Foerschler, Dr. Gasca, Fr. Marcelino Andreu, Fr. Lopez de Ratenaga (who has made a meticulous study of the phenomena at Garabandal, and drawn up a very thorough report on the matter); I talked to Fr. Corta and to several of the visionaries' relatives, etc. I also saw Dr. Puncernau from Barcelona, and Dr. Ortiz from Santander. I had the opportunity of clearing up one or two points, and rounding off my data on Garabandal.

That evening, we went to the car in search of some cans of food for an improvised cold supper. Afterwards, beneath the star-strewn expanse of a beautiful night sky, we organized a rosary service, a sublime procession up to the pines. Fr. Luna led, and the responses were given in many different tongues by a large group of men and women. We recited all fifteen mysteries, and Fr. Luna gave a very beautiful sermon on the feast of Corpus Christi which we were commemorating that day, June 17th, speaking of the hopes that had brought us all together in that atmosphere of peace of mind and love of Our Lady.

When we returned down the mountainside to the village, the road, seen from above, looked like a rosary of lights. We descended to take a closer look at the long line of cars, stretching out of sight. In many of them, pilgrims were sleeping. At Garabandal, a car is indispensable, for it becomes rather like a small apartment, serving as a larder, kitchen and dormitory.

Next morning, the priests all said Mass. The church was packed all morning. That day, Conchita was the center of everybody's attention. Wherever she went, there the crowds followed her. She received Holy Communion from the hands of Fr. Marcelino Andreu, a missionary in

Conchita among the pilgrims. On the right Mr. Lomangino, a blind American whose faith brought him to Garabandal.

Formosa and brother of the late Fr. Luis. When Conchita came out of church, more than thirty photographers and movie-cameramen were standing at the ready on the churchyard wall. Conchita was at once surrounded by a large crowd, kissing her, giving her pious medals, asking her to relay their requests to the Vision ... In church all morning was a French priest, Fr. Pel, aged 87, a man renowned for his saintliness." Fr. Pel had followed the course of events at Garabandal for some time, and that morning he assured everyone who asked him that he expected to see an impressive ecstasy that night.

After lunch, the rumor spread that the visionary had had two summonses. Old Garabandal hands were surprised at the news, because the apparition announced was of the Angel, and the "llamadas" or summonses only came when the Blessed Virgin appeared. I soon found that it was a false alarm, the result of someone's impatience, and perhaps not devoid of questionable intentions. Conchita, who was talking calmly with everybody who came near her, denied having had a summons.

The afternoon dragged on. People thronged the streets saying the rosary in different languages. People from France, Germany, Britain, Italy, Poland, the United States, etc., gathered before Conchita's humble dwelling, all unified by a common sentiment of supplication and love towards the Virgin Mary. Personally, I expected the apparition to take place in the early evening. I assumed that, as the Angel had appeared for the first time at 8:30 p.m., four years earlier, the prodigy announced would occur at more or less the same hour. I made for the center of the village and walked down the road to check the points of origin of the vehicles parked there. The result confirmed the sad truth: there were more foreign cars than Spanish ones. Garabandal is far better known outside Spain than within her frontiers. Is this perhaps due to the Church's attitude and the great respect felt in Spain for the decision of the ecclesiastical hierarchy? Otherwise, why would the events of Garabandal be so closely followed by Catholics all over the world, while Catholics in Spain remain ignorant, indifferent and silent?

I talked to Fr. Bernardino Cennamo, from the Convent of San Pasquale at Benevento (Italy). He gave me some photographs of Padre Pio, and as a relic, a scrap of cloth soaked in the blood from his stigmata. I met Roman journalist Gabriela Montemayor, and a famous Italian Television star, *Signor* Carlo Campanini. I spent some time with Fr. Pel, and with the apostle of Garabandal in France, Fr. Laffineur. I saw Dr. Caux, of whom we spoke in the chapter relating the miraculous Communion; and *Monsieur* Jean Masure, for whom Our Lady had a surprise in store that night, and he explained to me how, when he reached Torrelavega, he was on the point of turning back to Madrid because a priest assured him that Garabandal was a myth that had been condemned by the Church.

Towards 8:30 p.m., the hour that I had erroneously forecast for the ecstasy, I made my way to Conchita's house. The crowd were still standing or kneeling before her house, praying or singing hymns in Our Lady's honor. It was a most impressive sight. It must have been about ten o'clock when Conchita declared:

"The apparition will be a little later on, up at the sunken lane. Tell everyone to go on saying the rosary and doing penance. I'll be along in a short while."

The warning was spread in different languages. The crowd thinned rapidly as people went to find a good vantage-point in the lane where the children had had their first visions. This enabled me to reach Conchita's house. Her brother, who was standing guard at the door, invited me in. There, in the kitchen, humble yet welcoming as few kitchens can be, Conchita was sitting by the window, talking through its bars to the pilgrims outside.

I approached her. She sensed my concern and smiled. She was as calm as ever.

"There isn't much of the day left. Do you know everything that is going to happen," I asked, worried at the general disappointment if the expected did not occur.

"Yes, I don't know what the Angel will say to me, but I know all the rest of the details."

She looked at her watch, and added: "There's a little time to wait yet."

And she began to write little dedicatory notes on holy pictures, showing more signs of gaiety than of impatience.

It was then that I noticed the wedding rings that she was wearing on her fingers, and I asked if I could give her mine, too. But she at once explained: "Not today. The Angel doesn't kiss them . . ." And she laughingly added, "The Angel isn't anybody . . ."

She then wrote on a holy picture for Fr. Luna, a surname which in Spanish means "Moon". Wearing her best air of innocent mischief, she inquired:

"Shall I put Fr. Moon or Fr. Sun?"

All at once she was serious. She glanced at her watch and declared: "It's half-past eleven. Let's go to the lane."

Her mother—an admirable woman for whom the apparitions have been the cause of particular trials and suffering, and who treats pilgrims with extraordinary patience and kindness—got out a short jacket. Conchita put it on and, taking her cousin's arm, went out escorted by her brothers, by a few village lads, and by a large group of Civil Guards.

The Confirmation of Garabandal

I wanted to stick to the group escorting Conchita, but I was unable to. At once, an avalanche of people prevented my following close behind her. Hundreds of lights flashed from the shadows to light the way. Conchita broke into a run. She drew farther and farther away from me. We all entered the sunken lane jammed shoulder to shoulder. Suddenly, this human wave halted, wavering dangerously. Some fell to the ground. Spotlights flashed on, operated by technicians of the Spanish newsreel company NODO, and the Italian Television. As best I could, I clung to the wall of the lane and, after some effort, managed to scale it. I succeeded in reaching the top and leaning forward, I could see Conchita some distance below. On reaching the center of what is known as the *"cuadro"*, Conchita had fallen to her knees in a rapture.

Conchita in ecstasy, and the crowd on June 18, 1965 (see text).

I saw her with her eyes wide open and unblinking, receiving the full glare of the spotlights and flashbulbs. Her face was transfigured; it seemed transparent. Tape recorders were recording part of her celestial colloquy: "No, no, not yet ... " said Conchita pleading in that low, rather husky tone of voice which she has in ecstasy. All of a sudden, she raised her hand, in which she

167

bore a crucifix. She held it out at the Vision's command for Fr. Pel to kiss. I still have no idea how Fr. Pel managed to arrive at the forefront of the crowd. Afterwards, she held it out to one of Fr. Pel's companions, and finally to *Monsieur*Jean Masure, a Frenchman residing in Madrid. To him she later said:

"The Angel says I'm to tell you that the Blessed Virgin has granted your request."

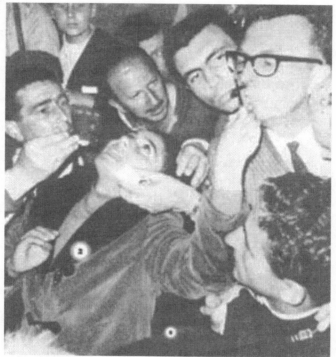

Conchita in ecstasy gives the Crucifix for M. Masure to kiss.

The ecstasy was breathtaking, and lasted some twenty minutes. Without warning, she rose to her feet and then crashed, like lead to the ground, her knees smashing onto the sharp stones in the lane. A grinding crunch was heard, like the sound of two stones being struck together hard. Nevertheless, it was afterwards seen that she had not come to the slightest harm.

She proceeded to make the Sign of the Cross in the customary way, and then emerged from her trance. At that instant, her eyes, which had unblinkingly withstood those torrents of light for twenty minutes, squeezed tight shut, and she covered her face with her hands to protect her eyes from the glare.

Had the visionary not been in a real trance, her open eyes, which withstood the concentrated beams of so many spotlights, would have been burnt out in a matter of minutes, and, today, Conchita Gonzalez would be blind. On the contrary, she came to quite normally, without being dazzled at all, and her eyes are as expressive and healthy as ever.

The dense crowd made it practically impossible for Conchita to retrace her steps down the lane. The Civil Guard and several village youths protected her from the buffeting as best they could, forcing a path through the tightly packed crowd. Several people slipped and fell as they scrambled down the lane, and those behind stumbled over them. A voice was heard calling for help. I felt a sudden fear, thinking of the possible consequences of that human avalanche. But, once again, the miraculous happened; quite inexplicably, there were no casualties.

I reached Conchita's house and managed to squeeze through the door. She answered our questions with that natural air of one who cannot see the importance of the phenomena in which she is playing a leading role.

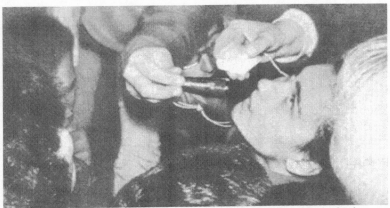

Scenes from the ecstasy of June 18, 1965, recorded and televised.

"The Angel has given me a message for the world."

"Can you tell us what it is?"

"No, not now."

"Is it good or bad?"

"What comes from God is always good."

"I mean, is it pleasant or unpleasant?"

She shrugged her shoulders.

"Can't you tell us straight away," I insisted.

"He told me to give it out in writing."

"Will we know what it is tomorrow?"

"Yes."

Watching the rapture had left us with an immense inner joy, and this, I could see, was general. That night, there was many an embrace and many a kind word of friendship between complete strangers. It was in this same spirit that I found myself embracing Fr. Bernardino Cennano, a Franciscan who had come from Italy.

In my view, the ecstasy of June 18th was the confirmation of Garabandal. Let us analyze the facts.

Conchita had a rapture on New Year's Day. She was alone. Two young shepherd boys saw her in ecstasy. By the time they had run to inform people in the village and had started back up the mountainside to see her, Conchita was descending the lane. Taken by surprise, she had no alternative but to tell her story.

"I saw Our Lady, and She told me the Angel is going to appear to me on June 18th, to give me a new message."

The news spread round Spain like wildfire, across the frontier and throughout the Catholic world. With her usual naturalness when recounting her visions, Conchita confirmed the news to everyone who asked. She calmly awaited the day announced by the Vision. She never lost her assurance and gaiety. She allayed my own fears, saying that she "knew all the details". At the time set for the Angel's apparition, she happily set off for the appointed place. And, the instant she reached the spot, she went into a rapture. Doctors checked that her trance and state of ecstasy were genuine. The powerful spotlights did not harm her eyes; her face was transfigured; her breathing and voice acquired the measure and tone proper to a state of ecstasy. All of a sudden, she rose to her feet and then crashed back, to her knees, a jarring blow that left her skin without so much as a graze. After twenty minutes, she emerged from her trance in a totally normal state. She spoke of a message that she would communicate in writing, and this message, composed by a young girl lacking anything more than the most elementary schooling, proved to be a piece of perfect theology. Is all this not clear proof of the supernatural causes of the phenomena we are relating?

The Message of June 18th, 1965

Late the next morning, after Mass, Conchita issued the message, written in her clumsy handwriting and poor spelling on a sheet of ordinary writing paper. Fr. Luna read it out in Spanish, French and Italian from the doorway of the visionary's home; Fr. Marcelino Andreu afterwards repeated it in English. The public who had been waiting for this moment heard the message in silence; many had tears in their eyes. Afterwards, they asked to be allowed to copy the text. Slowly, it was dictated in different languages, so that everyone could note it down correctly. Then, I was handed the message and held it up so that it could be photographed.

The message read as follows:

"The Message which the Blessed Virgin has given to the world through the intercession of St. Michael.

The Angel said: 'As my Message of the 18th of October has not been complied with, and as it has not been made known to the world, I am telling you that this is the last one. Previously, the Cup was filling; now, it is brimming over. Many priests are following the road to perdition, and with them they are taking many more souls. Ever less importance is being given to the Holy Eucharist. We should turn the wrath of God away from us by our own efforts. If you ask His forgiveness with a sincere heart. He will pardon you. I, your Mother, through the intercession of St. Michael the Archangel, wish to tell you that you should make amends. You are now being given the last warnings. I love you very much, and I do not want your condemnation. Ask Us sincerely and We shall grant your plea. You must make more sacrifices. Reflect on the Passion of Jesus.

Conchita Gonzalez, 18-VI-65."

A number of ideas can be gathered from this Message: Our Lady is disturbed at the lack of response to her message of October 18th, 1961; she is concerned about priests; the Holy Eucharist must be given the pride of place It deserves; it is essential that we appease God by our efforts . . . Our Lady promises forgiveness to those who ask for it sincerely; she tells us she *will grant us our pleas;* she insists that she loves us very much and desires our salvation; she asks us to make sacrifices and recommends us to reflect on the Passion of Jesus; she assures us that we are being given the last warnings, and that *this is the last message.*

All this fits in perfectly with the contents of the prophesies, and with the theological facts.

The ecstasy, announced almost six months earlier, and the contents of the message revealed to the child while in her trance are confirmation of the Garabandal apparitions for any Christian of good faith.

But such confirmation is not sufficient for the world at large, and much less for the Church, whose prudence is even more exacting. This is why Our Lady has announced what will be the final confirmation; namely, the public miracle whose date will be given beforehand, a miracle so spectacular that it will make any doubt impossible.

Time and again, when her visionaries have protested at the lack of faith of so many people, Our Lady has reassured them, saying that "they will believe in time . . ."

Faced with this mystery, however, our attitude meanwhile should be one of respectful and hopeful attention. To twist things around in an effort to elude a logical approach to the matter is neither wise nor just. Garabandal is crying out for a conscientious study of the facts by experienced specialists with good faith, *a study that has yet to be carried out.*

The Press Reports

It was with real surprise, if not a little annoyance, that we read in the Press a note from Santander, released by the "Cifra" News Agency to most Spanish newspapers. This report carried the headings "Alleged Apparitions in a village of the Province of Santander," and "The Ecclesiastical Hierarchy does not accept the possibility of supernatural causes." The full report read as follows:

"Circulars and pamphlets published in France have been the cause of the revival of the now old subject of the alleged apparitions in the **(continues page 174)**

El mensaje que la Santísima Virgen ha dado al mundo por
la intercesión del angel San Miguel!
    El Angel ha dicho!: Como ono se ha cumplido y ono se ha hecho
conocer al mundo omi mensaje del 18 de Octubre, os digo que
este es el ultimo.
Antes la Copa estaba llenando ahora este rebosando.
Los sacerdotes van muchos por el camino de la perdicion y
con ellos llevan a ominchas omas almas
La Eucaristia cada vez se da omenos importancia.
Devemos evitar la ira de Dios sobre onosotros, con onuestros es-
fuerzos.
Si le pedis perdon con ouestras almas sinceras, El os perdonará.
Yo, ouestra Madre, por intercesion del angel San Miguel, os
quiero decir que os enmendeis, Ya estais en los ultimos avisos,
os quiero omucho y ono quiero ouestra condenacion.
Pedidselo sinceramente, y Nosotros, os lo daremos.
Deveis sacrificaros omás. Pensad en la Pasion de Jesus
Conchita Gonzalez   18-VI-1965

"The Message which the Blessed Virgin has given to the world
through the intercession of St. Michael.

The Angel said: 'As my Message of the 18th of October has not been
complied with, and as it has not been made known to the world, I am
telling you that this is the last one. Previously, the Cup was filling; now,
it is brimming over. Many priests are following the road to perdition, and
with them they are taking many more souls. Ever less importance is being
given to the Holy Eucharist. We should turn the wrath of God away from
us by our own efforts. If you ask His forgiveness with a sincere heart, He
will pardon you. I, your Mother, through the intercession of St. Michael
the Archangel, wish to tell you that you should make amends. You are
now being given the last warnings. I love you very much, and I do not
want your condemnation. Ask Us sincerely and We shall grant your plea.
You must make more sacrifices. Reflect on the Passion of Jesus.
Conchita Gonzalez, 18-VI-65."

village of San Sebastian de Garabandal, where more than a thousand people, foreigners for the most part, gathered last Friday.

"A hundred and forty automobiles with foreign plates were counted and a bare fifty from various provinces of Spain; very few people from Santander went to the village.

"According to information given to us by a spokesman for the Chancery, the question of these alleged visions is far from new: it had already come up in 1961, when, on August 26th, to be exact, the Apostolic Administrator of the diocese. Dr. Doroteo Fernandez, signed an episcopal decree in which he said that, following investigations carried out in the matter by a Commission appointed for the purpose, "nothing obliges us to confirm the supernatural origin of the events." This decree also said: 'It is our desire that priests, be they of this or any other diocese, and religious of both sexes, even the independent clergy, should FOR THE TIME BEING abstain from going to San Sebastian de Garabandal.'

"The same Apostolic Administrator again addressed the members of his diocese on October 19th of the same year, saying that 'it would show a great lack of sense on our part if we were to accept as coming from God any gust of the wind of human opinion.' There is no proof that the said apparitions, visions, locutions or revelations can so far be presented as true and authentic, or be held as such on any serious grounds." This decree insisted on the prohibition imposed on priests, and asked them to inform the faithful of the true attitude of the Church in these matters.

"Again, a year later, on October 7th, 1962, the Feast of the Holy Rosary, the Bishop of Santander, Mgr. Eugenio Beitia Aldazabal, signed a further episcopal decree whose provisions read as follows:

'We fully confirm the official notes issued by this Chancery and dated August 26th and October 19th, 1961.'

'We forbid all priests, be they of this or any other diocese, and all religious, even the independent clergy, to gather at the aforesaid village without express permission from the diocesan authorities.'

'We repeat to the faithful the warning that they should abstain from going to this village for the purpose of heightening the atmosphere of excitement created by the unfolding of these events'

"Regarding this year's recurrence of the alleged apparitions, for the reasons indicated above, the attitude of the Chancery (so the spokesman informs us) remains unchanged. It is thought scientifically possible that the fourteen year old child who claims to see the apparitions may be suffering from a condition of health conducive to ecstatic trances, but all this is of a natural order, and there is no possibility of any supernatural cause."

174

It is hard to believe that this note, which contains errors and contradictions by the dozen, was really issued by a spokesman of the Chancery of Santander. It is far more likely to have been the product of a journalist's hasty pen.

In it we are told that the "circulars and pamphlets published in France have been the cause of the revival of the now old subject of the alleged apparitions," whereas, in fact, it should be the other way round. The inexplicable phenomena that have occurred and still are occurring at Garabandal are the one and only cause of the circulars, pamphlets and books published in France, Spain and elsewhere. What is more, it is quite obvious to everybody that, if people from many countries gathered at Garabandal on June 18th, it was not because pamphlets were published in France, but because the visionary, who has so often proved to be right in her predictions, had announced for that day an apparition of the Angel for a particular purpose. And this prophesy, like all her others, was fully confirmed when the time came.

In the second place, the note takes great pride in stating that most of the cars that went to Garabandal were from abroad, while very few people from Santander itself went to the village. We, modestly, beg to think otherwise. It is a disgrace to Spain and particularly to Santander that, notwithstanding the favor shown in the mere possibility of our land being chosen as the scene and our nation as the emissary of God's manifestations, we should have cloaked in silence what may well prove to be a great and unique task in the history of mankind.

The news agency report gives the visionary's age as fourteen, whereas, in fact, she was sixteen at the time.

It further denies the supernatural origin of the apparitions, claiming to confirm the episcopal decrees hitherto published. But the truth of the matter is that, as we have seen, those decrees go no further than adopting a prudent approach, repeatedly stressing that *for the time being* there is no definite proof of the supernatural origin of the events . . . The decrees do not close the door to future evidence, or use the tone of denial and condemnation so blatantly employed in the news agency note.

The news agency states that priests are forbidden to go up to Garabandal. This is not true either. The episcopal decrees simply dictate that *"they should not go there without prior permission."* This stipulation is merely for the purpose of controlling their movements, but not of generally prohibiting their going.

Finally, the note claims that "it is thought scientifically possible for the fourteen year old (?) child who claims to see the apparitions to be suffering from a condition of health conducive to ecstatic trances, but all this is of a natural order and there is no possibility of any supernatural cause."

This paragraph can be divided into two parts, both equally inadmissible. The first is the recognition of the fact that the child has genuine raptures; a surprising admission this, when it is considered that no steps have been taken either to study their causes or to classify them from a medical viewpoint.

We are to assume that the child is calmly left to fend for herself, without any medical assistance whatsoever; and without any prior investigation of the matter, the note declares that the ecstasies are of a natural order. This is the first incongruous point.

The second is far more serious. The second part makes the following allegation, no less: (we quote, word for word, the second heading of the news agency report, just as it appeared in the *"Heraldo de Aragón"* of Saragossa, on June 20th).

"The ecclesiastical hierarchy does not accept the possibility of any supernatural cause."

Quite honestly, I think it is a bit much that the ecclesiastical hierarchy should claim to limit God's activities by denying the possibility of his supernatural intervention whenever He pleases. I think that at Garabandal, or anywhere else for that matter, the ecclesiastical authorities have no alternative but to admit the possibility of God making manifestations to mankind as and when He thinks fit.

All those who are convinced that something of the greatest importance is going on at Garabandal have come to this conclusion after a meticulous and cautious investigation of the facts. It would be indiscreet on my part to reveal names, but I can assure the reader that leading doctors, very prudent theologians and the most expert specialists have been to Garabandal and are definitely inclined to affirm the existence of something that is, scientifically speaking, inexplicable.

How can the special Commission, referred to by the Chancery of Santander in some of its decrees, take such an uncompromising negative attitude? This we do not know. We can only say, for the reader's information, that other people also carried out an investigation with the permission of the Chancery, and they reached the opposite conclusion.

Perhaps it is all due to the desire of some well-meaning people to create obstacles for the sake of prudence, and thus force Our Lady's hand so that her miracle will be even more spectacular and conclusive. The layman does not understand these tactics. Nor dare he criticize them. He respects them in all sincerity because he realizes that, if the phenomena at Garabandal are confirmed, as we expect them to be, then Mary's triumph will be all the greater, the Church will have given us an admirable lesson in holy prudence, and God's enemies will have no grounds for their attacks which customarily speak of "comedies artfully arranged in advance with the help of the clergy."

And, if the phenomena are not confirmed, the Commission in question will have rendered the Church its greatest service.

Let us then leave the issue of Garabandal open and wait till Heaven and future events, which will speak more eloquently than we can, bring the issue to its close. For the time being, and in a spirit of respectful anticipation, we shall continue to put our trust in the Virgin Mary; we shall humbly pray Her to enlighten our minds and to kindle the flame in our hearts, so that we may fulfill the Message, by making it the guide of our life and the source of inspiration of our apostolate

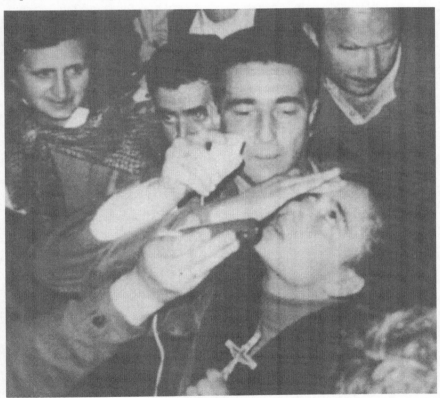

REPERCUSSIONS

On July 8th, 1965, the Bishop of Santander, Mgr. Eugenio Beitia Aldazabal, issued a note which stated, among other things: "We hereby declare that We have not found any matter deserving condemnatory ecclesiastical censorship, either in the doctrine or in the spiritual recommendations that have been divulged on this occasion as having been addressed to the Christian faithful, for these recommendations contain an exhortation to prayer and sacrifice, to devotion to the Holy Eucharist, to veneration of Our Blessed Lady in traditional praiseworthy ways, and to holy fear of God, offended by our sins. They simply repeat the common doctrine of the Church in this respect."

The note goes on to say that "the Chancery has collected a large amount of documentary evidence in the last few years with regard to everything that has occurred. *Its dossier on this issue has not been closed.* It will always be grateful to receive all evidence sent in. The Supreme Sacred Congregation of the Holy Office has entered into contact with the diocese of Santander to obtain information on this grave matter."

In our desire to cooperate within our modest means and ever at the service of the Church and the ecclesiastical hierarchy, the author is sending this book to the open dossier at the Chancery of Santander. All the evidence contained in this volume has been checked and re-checked, over and over again; and in Spain, only a limited edition has been published for specialists and followers of events at Garabandal.[†] It is to be hoped that this work may serve as yet another item of evidence in the Garabandal dossier, which is now beginning to be studied thoroughly and objectively.

In so doing, I feel I am making my own very modest contribution, while at the same time complying with the dictates of my conscience, which, because of circumstances of personal significance, I could not possibly ignore.

◆ ◆ ◆

[†] We hope that Heaven will send confirmation of the supernatural causes of the phenomena at Garabandal, so that we may apply for the "Imprimatur" and publish the book on a scale that the subject deserves.

ROME AND THE LAST APPARITION

We have thought it worthwhile to add to this new edition a chapter relating the latest events connected with Garabandal: Conchita's trip to Rome, and her vision on November 13th, 1965.

At the same time, and in view of the importance of the visionary's assertions of a prophetic nature—namely, all she has said about the Warning, the Miracle and the Punishment—we give below three notes written by Conchita herself, in which she explains everything she knows about these points. These notes will enable the reader to see for himself the importance and the plausibility of the prophesies.

The notes read as follows:

THE WARNING—"The Virgin told me about this on January 1st, 1965, up in the pine grove. I cannot say what it will consist of, because she did not command me to do so. And, as for when it is going to be, she did not tell me, so I do not know. What I do know is that it will be visible to everybody; it will be a direct work of God and will take place *before the miracle*. I do not know whether people will die because of it. They could only die from the shock of seeing it."

THE MIRACLE— "The Virgin told only me about the miracle. She forbade me to say what it will consist of. I cannot reveal the date either until eight days beforehand. What I am allowed to say is that it will coincide with an event in the Church, and with the feast of a saint who is a martyr of the Holy Eucharist; it will be at half-past eight on a Thursday evening; it will be visible to everybody in the village and on the surrounding mountainsides; the sick who are present will be cured and the incredulous will believe. It will be the greatest miracle that Jesus has worked for the world. There will not remain the slightest doubt that it comes from God and is for the good of mankind. In the pine grove, a sign of the miracle will be left forever. It will be possible to film and televise it."

THE PUNISHMENT—"The punishment is conditioned to whether or not mankind heeds the Blessed Virgin's messages and the miracle. If it does take place, then I know what it will consist of, because the Virgin told me, but I am not allowed to say. What is more, I have seen the punishment. What I can assure you is that, if it comes, it is far worse than if we were enveloped in fire; worse than if we had fire above us, and fire beneath. I do not know how long a time will elapse after the miracle, before God sends it."

We have in our possession the original copies of these texts, in Conchita's own handwriting.[†]

A Letter from Conchita about Her Last Vision (November 13th, 1965).

Conchita's letter about her vision of November 13th reads as follows:

"The Virgin has announced to me in a locution while I was in church that I would see her in the pine grove on Saturday the 13th of November; a special apparition to kiss religious objects to be distributed afterwards, because they are of the greatest importance.

"I longed for that day to arrive, so I could once again see those who have brought the felicity of God to my soul; namely, the Blessed Virgin with the Infant Jesus in her arms.

"It was raining that day, but of course I did not mind going up to the pines; with me, I had a lot of rosaries that had recently been given me so I could hand them out. As the Blessed Virgin had told me, I took them with me so she could kiss them.

"While I was on my way up to the pines alone, I said to myself that, since I was very repentant about my faults, I would not commit any of them again, because I felt ashamed of presenting myself before the Mother of God without first ridding myself of them.

"When I reached the pines, I started to take out the objects that I had with me, and at that instant I heard a very sweet voice (the Blessed Virgin's, of course, which can easily be distinguished from any other voice) calling me by my name. I answered: 'What is it?' And, then, I saw her, with the Infant Jesus in her arms; she was attired as usual and smiling. I said to her, 'I've come to bring you the rosaries for you to kiss.' She said to me: 'So I see.'

"I had been eating chewing-gum, but the moment I saw the Blessed Virgin, I stopped chewing and stuck it behind a tooth. But, she obviously must have known that I had it there, and she said to me: 'Conchita, why don't you give up your chewing-gum and offer it up as a sacrifice for the Glory of My Son.' I felt ashamed, and taking it out I threw it on the ground. And she said to me:

[†] *IMPORTANT NOTE*—The printing of this book was almost completed when there came into my hands a prophesy by Sister Maria Faustina, a Polish nun who died during the invasion of Poland in 1938. The prophesy was written on February 22nd, 1931, and reads as follows:

"The Lord manifested Himself to me today, and He said to me: 'Before coming as the just Judge, I shall come as the King of Mercy. Before Judgment Day arrives, there will appear a sign in the heavens and over the earth. That sign will be the Sign of the Cross, and from each of the wounds in My hands and in My feet there will issue a bright light that will illumine the whole earth for a few minutes. This will be the end of time'."

Could this be a prediction of the great miracle of Garabandal, announced way back in 1931 ?

'You will remember what I told you on your saint's day, that you will suffer very much on earth; well, I repeat it to you, once again. Have trust in Us, and you will bear it with pleasure for Our Hearts, and for the good of your brethren, and thus you will feel Us closer to you.'

"I said to her: 'How unworthy I am. Our Mother, of so many graces received through you, and even so you have come to me today to lighten the little Cross which I now bear.' She said to me: *'Conchita, I have not come only for your sake; I have come for the sake of all my children,* with the desire of bringing them closer to Our Hearts.' And she then asked me: 'Give me everything you have brought for me to kiss.' I gave everything to her. With me I had a Crucifix; she kissed that, too, and said to me: 'Pass it through the hands of the Infant Jesus.' I did so. He did not say anything to me. I said to the Blessed Virgin: *'I shall take this Crucifix to the convent with me.'* She did not say anything. After kissing everything, She said to me: 'Through the kiss that I have bestowed on them, My Son will work prodigies. Distribute them to others.' 'Of course I shall do so.'

"She told me to tell her the petitions that others had requested me to convey to her. I told her, and she said: 'Tell me, Conchita, tell me things about my children; I have all of them beneath my mantle.' I said to her: 'It is very small, we cannot fit them all in.' She smiled.

'Do you know, Conchita, why I did not come myself on June 18th to give you the message for the world? Because it saddened me to tell it to you myself. But, I have to tell you it for your own good, and, if you all fulfill it, for the Glory of God. I love you all very much, and I desire your salvation and to gather you all here in Heaven, around the Father, Son and Holy Spirit. You will respond to me, Conchita, won't you?' And I said to her: 'Yes; if I were to see you all the time, yes, I would. But if not, I do not know, because I am very bad.' 'You do your best, and We shall help you.'

"She only stayed a short time, and she also said to me: *'This is the last time you will see me here,* but I shall always be with you, and with all my children.' Afterwards, she added: 'Conchita, why do you not go more often to visit My Son at the Tabernacle? Why let yourself be overcome by laziness, not going to visit Him, when He is there waiting for you all *day and night?"*

"As I said before, it was raining, and the Blessed Virgin and the Infant Jesus did not get wet at all. While I saw them, I did not notice that it was raining, but, afterwards, when I saw them no longer, I was all wet. I had said to the Blessed Virgin: 'How happy I am when I see you. Why do you not take me with you now?' She said to me: 'Remember what I told you on your saint's day, and when you present yourself before God you must show Him your hands full of good works done by you for the benefit of your brethren and for the Glory of God; and at present your hands are empty.'

"And that was all. The joyous moment passed when I was with my Mama in Heaven, my best friend, and the Infant Jesus. I saw Them no longer, but I did not cease to feel Them. Once again, They left my soul full of peace, joy and a great desire to overcome my faults and to love with all my strength the Hearts of Jesus and Mary Who love us so much.

"Earlier, the Blessed Virgin told me that Jesus would not send us the Punishment to harm us, but to help us, and to reprove us for not heeding Him; and the Warning, to purify us to make us see the Miracle through which He shows us the great love that He bears us and, hence, His desire" for us to fulfill the message.

"We should do our very best for the Glory of God and our Blessed Mother.

"This is the apparition of November 13th, a Saturday, to Conchita Gonzalez.

P.S. This is not a secret."

The letter is admirable from start to finish: the naive, childish detail about her chewing-gum; Our Lady's assertion that she has not come for the children's sake, but for that of all mankind, always answering with a smile and not paying too much attention to the visionaries' personal problems (this is a circumstance in favor of the supernatural origin of these events, particularly in the case of Conchita's desire to take the crucifix passed through the Infant Jesus' hands to the convent with her, which was a wily attempt to sound the Blessed Virgin out on a matter that is currently Conchita's cross and prime cause of concern); the visionary's reply to the Blessed Virgin's interest in her children, "all of whom she has beneath her mantle", an ironical sally that brought a smile to Our Lady's lips; Our Blessed Mother's affectionate explanation of why she delivered her message of June 18th through an intermediary, a point which fully reveals the loving kindness with which she treats her children; Conchita's fears of "not living up to the graces which she receives" if she is not fortunate enough to go on seeing the Blessed Virgin, because she considers herself "bad"; Our Lady's promise that she will be attentive to all her children's needs; the fact that Jesus is waiting for us night and day in the tabernacle; and the highly important revelation that this is the last apparition for Conchita at Garabandal, which indicates that the Virgin will continue to keep in touch with her visionary, but away from what has so far been the scene of these exceptional manifestations.

The Blessed Virgin did not want to "take Conchita with her" because her hands are *empty of good works*; we should all meditate on these words and ask Heaven to grant us, too, the grace to fill our hands and remain on earth until we have gathered sufficient merits so that we may leave this world with the satisfaction and joy of having done our duty. Conchita's "Mother and best Friend", as she calls her, left her filled with peace, joy and a desire to achieve perfection.

And, to encourage us in our daily toils, let us bear in mind one point. If, after seeing the Blessed Virgin so often, Conchita is still afraid of her imperfections, should she be left without Our Lady's apparitions and assistance, then, how much more justified such fears and errors are in the case of people who have not had the good fortune to see the reality of the supernatural world with their own eyes.

But, the Blessed Virgin has repeated time and time again that she comes for the sake of all mankind and all her children, and she has us all beneath her mantle; she "loves us all very much and desires our salvation." For, God is sending us the warning so there will be no further doubts about the miracle, and so that the greatest possible number of people may be present to see it; the miracle will be like a final effort to convert sinners and thus, as far as possible, avert Heaven's punishment.

Let us read this letter a thousand and one times, and draw from it the surprising spiritual fruits which it encloses.[†]

Conchita's Trip to Rome

The discretion advisable as regards Conchita's visit to Rome prevents our revealing full details of the circumstances and facts surrounding this pilgrimage. Consequently, let us simply say that she was summoned by Cardinal Ottaviani; that she requested and obtained The Holy Father's blessing for her subsequent entry into a convent; that she spent two and a half hours at the Congregation of the Holy Office, and that, at the request of those who accompanied her, she went to see Padre Pio We can also say that "everything went off very smoothly and was clearly providential, and there is reason to be very pleased and deeply grateful to God."

Rather than go to Rome, what Conchita really wanted to do was to come

---

[†] While Conchita was alone up in the pine-grove, receiving Our Lady's visit, a truck was climbing the steep mountain track leading up from Cosio to Garabandal, fell into a gorge and was completely wrecked. In the truck were many villagers who were returning from morning market in Puentenansa, There were no casualties. Everyone escaped unscathed from this spectacular accident.

back from Rome, because her mother, Aniceta, had promised her that, upon her return, she would allow her to go to the convent in Pamplona.

Circumstances Common to All Apparitions

I should like to stress the fact that some events that have taken place at Garabandal fully coincide with other similar ones which are proper to all the apparitions that have been officially approved by the Church. This is true of the characteristics of the ecstasies: the great weight very often acquired by the visionaries; total imperviousness to pain; the instantaneous fall to their knees as if their feet were swept from under them, a phenomenon that is typical of the different manifestations of this kind; the presence of an angel who prepares the visionaries and announces the Blessed Virgin's visit to them (Catherine Laboure, the children of Fatima, etc.); the summonses, which were similarly felt by Bernadette, who knew, in this way, when she had to go to the grotto; the secret which generally concerns mankind's punishment and which occurred in the case of Our Lady of Paris, La Salette and Fatima; the terminology used by the Blessed Virgin, etc., etc.

The Negative Note at Garabandal

The negative note at Garabandal is struck by Mary Cruz. The Church's justified attitude is no doubt due to her, but we should not overlook the fact that all the visions that have eventually turned out to be God's work have passed through a negative stage of confusion and controversy.

We ought not, in principle, to be surprised that a matter as delicate as the possible presence of the supernatural should be surrounded by a certain atmosphere of confusion and some contradictory aspects in which positive and negative arguments mingle at one and the same time. Such confusion justifies the Church's prudence and the fact that It has deferred final judgment until there is full confirmation in the form of a miracle. If there were no question mark hanging over Garabandal; if Garabandal were a clear, indisputable, proven affair, and if it had the Church's backing from the outset, then, faith in Garabandal would be entirely devoid of merit of any kind, and the reaction of the multitudes would make the normal course of its history impossible. If Conchita's statement about the curing of the sick who are present on the day of the miracle were believed out of hand by mankind *en masse,* on account of clear, unquestionable evidence of the reality of her assertion, then, the reader can picture what it would be like . . . The entire world would react and all mankind would strive to gather at a single geographical point; survival would be impossible. Divine Providence has, therefore, always permitted these prodigies to be surrounded by a certain air of confusion, contradictions and negative arguments, which are eventually cleared up by a spectacular miracle in the presence of a large number of people who are worthy of that grace. Only in this fashion can the human development of such events follow its proper course. It was not for nothing that Jesus Christ also spoke in parables in the Gospels.

Finally, we should add that Mary's apostolic activity is unceasing and encompasses the whole globe. Her activity begs a question:

On the day of the miracle at Garabandal, will the prodigy likewise take place simultaneously in all the places that have been, or are now, the scene of similar Marian manifestations?

We hope that this will indeed be the conclusion reached from the investigations we have mentioned, whose findings we shall publish in due course. The key-note of these investigations will be the location of the greatest possible number of present-day manifestations that are probably supernatural, for the purpose of comparing them with others, analyzing the contents of the respective messages and the promise of their confirmation in a public miracle. In principle, we do not consider it absurd to hold the view that such a miracle might take place at all those places chosen by Mary, at the same hour on the same day. From our survey it will be possible to see the geographical area covered by Heaven's activities, for there can be no doubt whatsoever that The Virgin Mary is making an all-out effort to save mankind through the use of a plan devised by Providence, and mankind is spread over many countries and continents. The voice of this Lady who appears surrounded by brilliant light will reach us all, casting the life-line of salvation to each people in its own language and according to its needs.

Through this documentation which we intend to gather, and for which we request and desire assistance from all those who can provide any information, it will be possible to weigh up the extent of Our Heavenly Mother's apostolic mission of love and effort.

In this study, we shall also deal with The Blessed Virgin's amazing activity in the heart of Russia.

Pilgrims reciting the rosary at the Pines with Loli and Conchita (August 1965).

APPENDIX A

OFFENSIVE TACTICS

3.—Monroy commences his book as follows: "I had always wanted to make known the contradictions of every kind that I had observed in the apparitions at Lourdes and Fatima as related in the books I had read. So, I decided to take the opportunity offered me by these four little Spanish girls who have come to make international headlines from their almost unknown upland village in the province of Santander."

That is how *"El Mito de las Apariciones"* begins. The author divides it into two parts; the first, dedicated to an account of events at San Sebastian de Garabandal, barely sticking to the facts at all, but doing his utmost to ridicule everything; the second part is an attempt to place other cases of apparitions on a par with Garabandal, the main targets being Lourdes and Fatima. The whole maneuver is painfully obvious. By convincing the reader of the fallacy of the apparitions at Garabandal, not yet sanctioned by the Church, it is easier to introduce a suspicion of fallacy in the case of other apparitions of the same order, even despite the guarantee offered to the sincere Catholic by the ecclesiastical sanction in such cases. Having thus shaken the foundations of the reader's faith in happenings accepted as true by the Church, it is a fairly simple matter to discredit the Church herself. Monroy has employed language which he himself admits in his preface to be "daring, tough, and even violent". He claims that this was unavoidable. "It is the natural reaction of a person who has lived with the very deceit that he now repudiates. It is not a question of hard language chosen to be offensive. It is the rebellion of a sincere thinker against religious divergence, against the collective suicide of the masses in the crafty hands of the Enemy. It is the righteous indignation of a suffering soul at the false spiritual shepherds who are leading the flock to perdition."[†]

The Angels are Acquitted ...

4.—Let us look at the contradictions mentioned by Monroy, on which he bases his case to make "as clear as daylight" the deceit behind the apparitions at Lourdes and Fatima.

He starts by attacking the fact that the visionaries at Fatima, like those at Garabandal, saw the Blessed Virgin, the occasional angel, and even the Infant Jesus and St. Joseph. This is quite beyond Monroy. Try as he may, he can find no plausible explanation, a fact which is hardly surprising since, rationally speaking, it is not easy to grasp. Indeed, we consider it miraculous precisely because it is not logically natural. Monroy, however, does give his blessing to the angels. "We have no objection," he says, "as far as angels are concerned. They can appear to human beings if God wills it, because we have precedents to prove it in the Bible. This does not mean that we admit their having appeared at Garabandal, Lourdes or Fatima. We repeat that they can appear if God sees fit. They are heavenly beings. They were not born and therefore they have not

---

[†] Monroy, "El Mito de las Apariciones." Editorial Pisga. Preface.

died; there is no angel's body on earth".[†] It can therefore be deduced that they can appear *"because they have not died"*.

Monroy takes the Holy Bible absolutely literally, and since the Bible includes two hundred and seventy-three instances (I quote his figures) of apparitions of angels, he has no doubts whatsoever on this matter. But he claims, on the other hand, that subsequent to the Incarnation of Jesus Christ and the descent of the Holy Spirit at Pentecost *"the ministry of the angels came to an end"*. According to Monroy, thenceforth God could not make use, however much He might wish to do so, of more than two means of convincing mankind: the Holy Spirit and the Holy Bible,[††]

In the light of his own appeals for a rational, comprehensible approach to the whole matter, his case would not appear to be watertight. But he ends with a triumphant flourish. "After having spoken His final word to mankind on the Grecian island of Pathmos, nearly two thousand years ago, God cannot conceivably be wasting His time in this turbulent age of ours sending us angels from heaven . . ." And it is all the more astonishing and unthinkable that He should send them "to innocent children who are of no specific use".[†††]

In Monroy's view, visions of angels are surprising, apparently impossible and highly absurd. Yet he does concede the point that they are just feasible. What he will not admit under any circumstances is the possibility of apparitions of the Infant Jesus, the Blessed Virgin or St. Joseph. Let us see why.

"What sort of body does Jesus have in heaven? The body of a man or of a child?" he asks. "His body, as the holy women saw Him after the resurrection, was the body of a man. The voice that threw St. Paul from the saddle and reproached him for his persecution was the voice of Christ the Man. In the thirteenth century, Raimyndo Lull claimed to have had a vision of Jesus Christ, and he saw Him as a man. In December 1954, Pope Pius XII told the world that Jesus had appeared to him, and here again, the vision was of a man. How is it that they saw Him in the form of a child at Fatima? Does Christ in heaven change bodies as we do shirts?"[††††] And, having expounded his views in this flippant and irreverent tone, he adds: "If He wants to, then of course He can. But ... to what purpose?"

As I understand it, it is Monroy who runs into contradictions here. After assuring us that only angels can appear in visions, he asserts the reality of a whole series of apparitions of Our Lord in order to refute those of the Infant Jesus.

The explanation of this phenomenon is given by a Dominican scholar, Fr. Antonio Royo Marin, a specialist in visions and — so Monroy makes out, although we ourselves have no evidence to support this — a staunch supporter of the events at San Sebastian de Garabandal. Monroy himself quotes Fr. Royo Marin as follows: "In one form or another, absolutely everything that exists may be the object of a supernatural vision; God, Jesus Christ, the Blessed Virgin, the angels, saints, souls in purgatory, devils,

---

[†]   Monroy; page 35
[††]   Monroy; page 35
[†††] Monroy; page 36
[††††] Monroy page 36

188

living beings and even inanimate objects." This is too much for Monroy, and the reason is only too clear. "These assertions", he counters, "lack any biblical basis". There is, nevertheless, one vision which is frequently quoted by spiritualists. It is a unique case that admits no argument because it is quoted from the Holy Bible. Monroy refers us to "Chapter XXVIII of the First Book of Samuel, where the prophet appears to King Saul. There is no doubt whatsoever that the vision was indeed Samuel and not a satanical trap, as some have attempted to make out. But this apparition tells us nothing since it was totally negative."[†]

Monroy sets about proving that it was a *negative* vision. "Firstly," he proceeds, "both the seer and King Saul were aware that they were breaking God's laws by invoking Samuel's spirit. Secondly, Saul did not consult the dead man in order to obtain a favor from God, but because he knew that he was not in His grace, but in the hands of the devil. Thirdly, as Samuel did not tell him what he wanted to know, Saul did not benefit by this vision. Fourthly, on the contrary, Samuel informed the king that he would die the following day for having committed the grievous sin of consulting the dead. And fifthly, Samuel complained to Saul at having been disturbed from his celestial repose."[††]

"This is the sole case in the whole Bible," concludes the author, "where we are told of a dead man appearing to a living being. And, as Dr. Pache says. God permitted this *unique* miracle to show us the tragic consequences of such apparitions."

In other words, when an innocent little girl claims that she has seen Our Lady, and thus succeeds in drawing large crowds, despite her being totally ignorant and lacking in any special ability or powers to stage a farce; when she promises a miracle six months in advance, as at Fatima, even foretelling the exact date and hour so that all may believe; when, at the appointed time, more than seventy thousand people gather—many with the idea of mocking at the failure of the prophesy—and witness the spine-chilling dance of the sun and all the other attendant phenomena; when another young girl kisses the ground and scrapes away some soil in obedience to the strange commands of the vision, and a spring bubbles forth from the spot, as at Lourdes, defying all droughts and curing the bodies and souls of hundreds of incurably sick people . . . etc.; when such things happen and are easily proved because they are recent occurrences, they do not give credence to the existence of a miracle since our reason cannot explain them. Whereas, on the other hand, what is quite plausible, easy to believe because it is in the Bible, is this prodigy of a man who died over two thousand years ago coming to life when invoked shortly afterwards by a living being whose soul had fallen into the hands of the devil. What strange powers of persuasion the Bible has over Mr. Monroy!

His attitude here, however, is such that simple logic at once refutes it. If, after studying each case, Monroy does not believe in the apparitions at Fatima or those at Lourdes, which are close in time to our own day and age, and are thus easily ascertained, then,

---

[†] Monroy Page 39
[††] Monroy Page 39

logically enough, he is even less likely to believe in King Saul's vision of Samuel, even though he may claim to do so in his book. And I only say this because I believe Mr. Monroy to be capable of normal, sensible thought.

The "Myth" of the Assumption

5. — Let us see what he has to say about St. Joseph and Our Blessed Mother.

"Tradition tells us that St. Joseph died in Jerusalem and the Blessed Virgin in Ephesus. According to the Catholic Church, the Virgin ascended body and soul into heaven immediately after her death. But the Bible makes no mention at all of this assumption . . ."* Thence, he deduces that it is all an invention on the part of the Catholic Church, inspired by a certain pagan ceremony with lanterns and candles, practiced by the Chinese "in honor of a mother who was rescued by her son from the power of death and the grave, this ceremony having been held in China from time immemorial."

Monroy is of the opinion that the Assumption of Our Blessed Mother into heaven is a tall story. "Mary and Joseph died, just as everyone else that is born has to die. In the presence of many witnesses, Mary was embalmed and buried. And nobody leaves the grave unless Christ commands it." He clarifies still further. "The bodies of these two saints were laid to rest in their tombs to await the glorious day of the Resurrection when, at a fanfare of God's celestial trumpets, the Lord Jesus will descend from heaven, and those who have died in Christ will rise again from the dead. Among those dead will be Mary and Joseph who, of course, *are now enjoying the divine presence* in that place of bliss which the Bible at one point calls Paradise, and at another point, Abraham's bosom."† And after this disclosure and concession by a man who is fully informed of all that goes on by reason of his profession as the editor of "La Verdad", the Christian reader sighs with relief, murmuring "Well! I'm glad to hear it!"

On page 40 in his book, Monroy enters into further details of the difficulties encountered by the souls of the departed in communicating with the world of the living. He ends the chapter as follows: "The dead have no means of communication with the living. The Virgin Mary died. St. Joseph died. They are both dead. And Catholic theologians tell us that the dead cannot return to this world. And since they cannot come here, the children at San Sebastian de Garabandal, at Lourdes and at Fatima, did not see the Virgin or St. Joseph, even though they may think they did. They were the dupes of the devil, as we shall have occasion to prove in due course, and the Catholic Church has served, and still is serving, as the instrument for the propagation of this piece of deception."††

---

† Monroy; Page 39
†† Monroy; Page 39

In the ensuing chapters, we shall see the ability of this "devil' to awaken piety in people, to draw crowds, to make sinners change their way of life, to make the faithful renounce the world and devote themselves to a life of prayer, sacrifice and penance. This is an amazing phenomenon of most effective apostleship; one that has occurred at Lourdes, Fatima and Garabandal, etc. But Monroy now proves to us that this splendid apostolate is not the work of God, or of the Blessed Virgin, or of the Infant Jesus, or of St. Joseph, or, for that matter, of the angels, but of the devil . . . The work of a poor devil whose every effort seems doomed to dismal failure; because, if he does not watch his step and goes on working so craftily and successfully, at this rate it will not be long before he is shocked to find colossal multitudes, totally deceived, being utterly transformed by their faith as a result of his "false apparitions" and taking the path of repentance and salvation. Blessed be an "enemy" who works in such a fashion.

Loli and Conchita saying the rosary.

Loli and Conchita at 16 (August 1965).

APPENDIX B

THE BEHAVIOR OF THE VISIONS

6.—"It is curious," says Monroy, "to note the nature of the instruments employed by the visions to achieve their ends. These instruments are invariably children between five and twelve years old." He adds: "Mary visited Bernadette at Lourdes and gave the Miraculous Medal to a charming little girl in Paris."

Before writing about apparitions, the first thing to do is to read up the case history of each one. If Monroy had taken the trouble to digest a little information, he would have seen that he was skating on very thin ice, because the "charming little girl" of Miraculous Medal fame was neither charming, in the ordinary sense of the word, nor a little girl. She was Sister Catherine Labouré, a Daughter of Charity aged twenty-one. Her vision took place in the chapel of the Daughters of St. Vincent de Paul in Boulevard Saint-Germain, Paris. In this case, the visionary was a physically and spiritually healthy nun with a normally developed intellect, and she was unlikely to fall into errors arising out of childish inexperience or, for that matter, out of hallucinations due to old age.

With a few exceptions, however, the fact is that the best known apparitions have been seen by young children. Why? Far be it from me to explain why Our Blessed Lady more often than not prefers children to adults when she wishes to give a message to mankind. In principle, I can see nothing contradictory in this fact. Nor do I find her choice in any way inappropriate.

In the first place, children have the advantage of their innocence, which makes them better prepared to receive so singular a grace. What is more, they transmit her message more accurately because, in their ignorance, they act automatically without their own intellect leading them to add or omit any detail of what they have seen or heard. Fr. Peyramale, the parish priest at Lourdes, did not believe in Bernadette's visions until, at his bidding, the child asked the Vision's identity. Bernadette came back with the answer: "She told me she was the Immaculate Conception". The young girl had never heard this expression in her life before, and, so that she should not forget it, she repeated it to herself over and over again, all the way back from the grotto at Massabielle to the parish priest's home.

On the other hand, adults sense the outcome of these events better, and realize the comment that they are bound to arouse. Experience has shown that adults are more cowardly when it comes to accomplishing the mission entrusted to them, afraid as they are of laying themselves open to public ridicule and scorn.

This is confirmed by the forerunner of the Marian apparitions. It took place on May 3rd, 1491, when the Blessed Virgin appeared to Thierry Schoere, a blacksmith at Orbey. Enveloped in a brilliant light. Our Lady held in her right hand three ears of wheat proceeding from a single stalk, while in her left hand there was an icicle.

The next few paragraphs are taken from "Estigmatizados y Apariciones". Here, before Monroy even took up his pen, was the reason why Mary's visionaries are generally children.

When Our Blessed Mother appeared, she addressed the blacksmith, saying: "My child, through their innumerable sins the people of these parts have aroused the divine wrath against themselves. The icicle which you see glistening in my left hand is a symbol of the hail storms, disease, famine and other punishments that are about to befall them. Nevertheless, my prayers have met with very special mercy and have thus far restrained the arm of my Son, already raised to punish them."

"If those who are to blame mend their ways and do penance. God will forgive them and bestow His Blessing and abundance on the land. This is the meaning of the stalk with three ears of wheat that I am holding in my right hand."

"In the name of these two symbols, go to Morwiller and tell the people what you have just seen and heard. Exhort them to flee from sin. Let them pray and, in turn, enjoin others to conversion. Otherwise, the heavenly punishments will not be long in coming."

The blacksmith then spoke to the Blessed Virgin. "My beloved Mother, I do not think these wicked people will believe my words."

"Most of them will believe your words". Our Lady replied, "if you make known to them the meaning of the icicle and the ears of wheat." The vision disappeared.

Trembling with excitement after his moving experience, the blacksmith made his way to Morwiller. He meditated on all that he had seen and heard, and on what he had to do. But, no sooner did he find himself in the presence of his neighbors than his courage failed him. He could not bring himself to mention his vision. Nobody would believe him; they would all laugh at him. Frightened at this thought, he prepared to make his escape while the going was good. He purchased a sack of corn and saddled his horse. About him were some of his neighbors. But, at that moment, a new prodigy took place. When he attempted to pick up the sack of corn, he found that he was unable to lift it. The bystanders laughed, and a few friends stepped forward to help him, jesting at his discomfiture. But, by this time, the sack had become so heavy that, strive as they might, they could not shift it an inch. All together, they made a final effort, but to no avail. The laughter died away. A strange foreboding took hold of them in the presence of the supernatural. Realizing the meaning of this second miracle, the blacksmith fell to his knees in their midst and confessed his guilt. So it was that he was forced by Our Blessed Mother to go through with the mission which his cowardice had led him to abandon. Perhaps this is why, from that time onwards, Mary discarded adults for revealing her messages and made use of children whose pure, unblemished souls were better able to accomplish difficult missions. All the children chosen as visionaries by Our Lady have done her bidding with heroic fidelity, even in face of those who seemed veritable executioners demanding the sacrifice of their lives. Such was the case with the children at Fatima, when threatened with death by the mayor of Ourem. This is the marvelous power of souls in a state of grace when confronted with seemingly insurmountable obstacles![†]

[†] Account quoted from "Estigmatizados y Apariciones", page 107 onwards.

The first message was essentially the same as those of Our Lady of Paris (1830), La Salette (1846), Lourdes (1858), Pontmain (1871), Fatima (1917), etc. Even the wording was the same. "My prayers have thus far restrained the arm of my Son . . ." These were the same words given to the children of Fatima and the other visionaries, all of which only goes to prove that there is not, and never has been, anything contradictory in the contents of the Marian messages. Indeed, in spite of the variable circumstances of time and location, they fully concur in their fundamentals and even in the expressions used.

Little "Messiahs" . . .

7.—Monroy sees a contradiction in the spirit of penitence which the Blessed Virgin impressed on the children, and which they actually practiced by offering up their sacrifices for the salvation of sinners.

"The children at San Sebastian de Garabandal," he says, "Bernadette at Lourdes, and the two girls and the little boy at Fatima, were all quite convinced that they had to suffer for the sake of sinners; in other words, that their physical and moral sufferings would be of benefit to the godless. They considered themselves little Messiahs, modern-age redeemers with vicarious sufferings in store for them. How ridiculous!" Here, as usual, Monroy has the Bible in mind where it says that "each of us shall account to God for himself", whence he claims that the offering of one soul to do reparation and suffer for another goes against biblical precepts. He then contradicts himself, saying that Christ has already "suffered for us", because, if nobody can suffer for the sake of another according to the Bible, then Christ could not do so for the sake of sinners. But Monroy sets aside the Bible at this point to take the easy way out. My sufferings are of no use to a fellow being because the Bible precludes it; Christ suffered for my sake, and this remission, on the other hand, is valid. Therefore, I need not bother my head about others any more than I need worry about my own salvation, which is guaranteed by the sufferings of the Savior.

What a pity it is that this comfortable, convenient doctrine has not been approved by the Church; it would get an enthusiastic reception!

But, Monroy indignantly resumes his train of thought. "The visions told the children that they should suffer for the sake of sinners. But God tells us in the Bible that this is not so, and that you cannot suffer for me any more than I, let alone those babes, can suffer for you; the reason being that Christ has already suffered for us; He suffered for all of us, for all time. So, where does the truth lie? Can twentieth century visions contradict Eternal God? Good heavens! How blind these priests are!"[†]

---

† Monroy; page 45

8.—Let us continue with what Monroy calls contradictions.

The Blessed Virgin said to the heavenly emissary who announced the mystery of the Incarnation: "Behold the handmaid of the Lord; be it done to me according to Thy word." These are words of sincere humility and are very revealing as to Mary's character. According to Monroy, this spirit of simplicity, submission and self-effacement is not in keeping with the language used by the Virgin when speaking to her visionaries, to whom she commonly gives directions in a somewhat authoritative tone. "It is incredible that people should be so blind as not to realize that the Virgin's words are highly presumptuous, and quite alien to the language of the Gospels; above all, these continual references to her Immaculate Heart. The real, one and only Mother of Jesus never said that she had been born 'immaculate,' says Monroy, on page 47 of this book.

There has undoubtedly been a great transformation in Mary, from the day when the archangel announced the Lord's choice, to what she is today as the Mother of God. In a pure, simple soul, her words of surprised submission at that moment were as logical then as it would be absurd, today, for her to appear to mankind and say that she was a nobody. It would be equally absurd for her, now, to speak without the authority proper, in heaven and on earth, to one who sets aside the laws of nature, becoming visible to human eyes at God's behest in order to deliver a message and issue instructions for our salvation. Jesus Christ Himself, fully aware of His identity and powers, did not hesitate to say: "I am the Way, the Truth and the Life . . ."; and He said that no-one could come to the Father except through Him. Nobody with a minimum of faith in the divine nature of Him who said these words would dream of denouncing them merely because they convey a certain authority which is incompatible with Monroy's concept of holy humility.

"And, as if this pack of lies were not enough," he goes on, "The vision at Fatima attributed to itself powers that belong to God alone. 'My Immaculate Heart will be your refuge and the path that will lead you to God . . . '; 'For your salvation, the Lord wishes to institute throughout the world the devotion to my Immaculate Heart . . .' Enough of this! Since when has the Virgin Mary been the refuge of sinners and the path leading sinners to God? Where does it say, in the Bible, that one can be saved through devotion to the heart of Mary? Does such a series of aberrations really come from the Virgin? Poor Mary!"[†]

Monroy is uncompromising in his interpretation of the Bible. He adamantly closes his eyes to the fact that two thousand years have elapsed; that God can complete His "official" revelations with other private ones; that the manifestations which He has since used to assist mankind are perfectly compatible with the authenticity of the Bible. He does not appear to see that the co-redemption by the Blessed Virgin gives her a leading role, and more than entitles her to take an active part in the salvation of the human race in such sad, difficult times. Since ancient times, there have been clear

---

[†] Monroy; page 50

references to this epoch of exceptional Marian apostolate. Our times were foretold by the prophets. We have always known that Mary would crush the serpent's head, and that a certain period in history was reserved for her, when she would intervene in person to show mankind the true road and save us from eternal damnation.

We live in the twentieth century. If Monroy wishes to meditate in all sincerity, he should cease his arbitrary interpretation of the Bible, and avoid the critical attitude he adopts in seeking a prefabricated, rational explanation for everything. In doing this, he does not hesitate to twist the facts themselves. He should simply contemplate those facts and, above all, expound them in all honesty. He should set aside the causes, which are far beyond our poor comprehension, and judge by the results. Then, he will see the prodigious, inexplicable, miraculous part of it all, and see the truth in the advice and messages, which are far from absurd or contradictory. There is certainly nothing absurd or contradictory in the Mother of God co-operating with her Son for the salvation of the world, and saying such simple things as these: "You must make reparation for your sins, which are disobedience of the laws of God, by means of repentance, prayer, penitence . . ." Fundamentally speaking, this is the sole content of all her messages. It is logical; the relationship between an infringement of the law and the ensuing punishment is a principle that automatically exists, even in Nature itself. In the words of Donoso Cortes: "It has been given to Man to bring society to its knees, to raze the strongest walls to the ground, to sack the most opulent of cities, to overthrow with a crash the farthest-flung empires, to bring horrifying ruin upon the most advanced civilizations, to behead kings or to defy reason. What has not been given to him is the power to suspend for a single day, for a single hour, for a single instant, the inescapable fulfilment of the fundamental moral and physical laws that constitute order in Mankind and in the universe; what the world has never seen, and never shall see, is Man, who flees from order through the gateway of sin, returning to order other than through the gateway of punishment and sorrow, that messenger from God who reaches all of us with His missives."[†]

There is nothing contradictory in Mary's messages. In fact, lest anyone should doubt that the message actually comes from her and think it a hallucination or the fruit of hysteria, in every case there have been extraordinary happenings to bear it out. Each message has been stamped with the divine hallmark of miracles. At Fatima, the miracle was announced six months in advance so that everyone should believe. And, at the appointed hour, the sun departed from its normal celestial path and fell earthwards within view of 70,000 spectators. Monroy would doubtless do well to consider this prodigy and then strike his breast and simply admit: "I cannot understand it because it is not in the Bible; but, in the light of what I have seen, I humbly believe . . ."

[†] Donoso Cortés. "Complete Works. Historical Sketches"; Vol. II, page 15.

Did Bernadette eat grass?

9. — Another of Monroy's arguments is that the vision has occasionally given the children strange commands. The apparition at Lourdes, for instance, "ordered Bernadette to go and 'drink and wash at the spring, and eat the grass that you will find there.' This is rather a strange message," says Monroy. "Anyone that thinks that God wastes His time telling little girls to eat grass has not the slightest idea who God is. And the story goes that the child obeyed these commands to the letter!!!"

But, that is not the story. Let us see what Bernadette herself had to say on the subject. On returning to the grotto, the day of the second apparition (February 14th), upon the advice of some of her neighbors, she went provided with holy water, in case it was an evil spirit. Bernadette was accompanied by Madame Millot and Madame Antoinette Peyret, their pencils and paper at the ready to note down whatever the vision had to communicate to them, for they thought it might be the soul of Madame Latapie, President of the Children of Mary, who had died recently. Our Lady smiled when asked to speak.

"It is unnecessary for you to write down what I have to say to you. Simply do me the kindness of coming here every day for the next fifteen days."

"What must I do?"

"Pray. Pray for sinners, for this troubled world. Do penance, penance. Tell the priests that I wish a chapel to be built here. I want them to come here. . . . Now, go to the spring and wash in it."

Bernadette's own account goes on: "As I could not see a spring, I went in the direction of the river Gave. The Lady called me and beckoned me to go to the grotto on my left. I obeyed, but I could not see any water at all. Not knowing where to get water from, I scooped away some earth and water began to flow from the spot. I allowed it to clear a little; then, I drank some and washed in it."

"Several times She repeated personal things to me, and told me they were for my ears alone, and that I was obliged to keep these things secret."

"I do not promise to make you happy in this world, but in the next," Our Lady said at one point.

"When she asked me to pray and do penance, she asked if I would not find it excessively unpleasant and tiring to climb the slope on my knees', kissing the ground. I replied, 'No'. Then, I embraced the ground . . ."

"Why?" they asked her.

"To do penance for myself and for others," she answered.[†]

From this version given by Bernadette, some have concluded that the child ate grass at the Virgin's orders. But this was not so. The Blessed Virgin wanted to leave behind on earth permanent evidence of her presence, namely, the miraculous spring at which so many pilgrims drink with total faith; the water in which the sick bathe, in which the viruses of an infinite number of diseases all mingle together without a single case of

---

[†] "Estigmatizados y Apariciones", page 133 onwards.

contagion being known, which is a miracle in itself. It is true that the Virgin commanded her to drink from a spring that she alone knew existed, and when the child could not find it, inspired her to scrape at the soil. It is certainly true that the water bubbled forth suddenly and the visionary drank from the spring, smearing the mud over her face. It is also true that the skeptics who witnessed the scene were disappointed at the triviality of this seemingly pointless procedure. I will even go so far as to allow what some other authors have stated, namely that Bernadette ate grass, and even that she did so at the command of the Virgin. In this way, the Virgin was able to put the visionary's spirit of obedience to the test. But the surprising part is not that she should have eaten grass or smeared her face with mud, or her embracing the ground as a sign of penitence. The true miracle lies in the fact that, when an ignorant child obeyed these orders, there issued from the hollow a trickle of water that grew and grew until, today, it produces 29,000 gallons a day. The miracle lies in the fact that this water has never ceased to flow and that it neither runs dry nor becomes brackish. And the cures . . .

Monroy should have dwelt on this point. After all, what would he say if he wrote an article in praise of Miguel de Cervantes, and I were to launch an indignant refutation of the author's fame, claiming that praise of Cervantes was absurd, because he had scrawled all over a few pieces of paper with a rude quill, getting his fingers inky in the process . . . An ignorant reader might come to the conclusion that I was right. But, my case would not, in fact, be valid, since I would have omitted the whole of the second part. And the second part is that Miguel de Cervantes scrawled with a quill-pen and smudged his fingers, but in doing so he left to posterity a work called "Don Quixote", which is considered a unique literary monument. His merit does not lie so much in getting ink all over his fingers, but in writing "Don Quixote". The difficulty in Bernadette's ease was not so much her eating grass, or smearing mud over her cheeks, but in her scraping away a little soil and bringing to light a spring that now produces 29,000 gallons of water a day, and survives all droughts and has hundreds of inexplicable cures to its credit.

If Monroy feels really ravenous one day and likes to try eating grass, and if, by so doing, he comes up with a similar achievement, let him notify me at once and I solemnly promise to write a book extolling his praises and to withdraw this work of mine from circulation.

Monroy lets fly

10.—In the next few chapters, Monroy claims that Purgatory is non-existent. This leads him to conclude that the apparitions at Lourdes and Fatima could not be real since the children spoke of a vision of Purgatory. He declares the emphasis on recitation of the rosary to be yet another contradiction, because the rosary is a pagan practice. He is struck by the fact that the Virgin should have taken part in the recitation of a rosary in her own honor,[†]

[†] At Garabandal, the Vision said the rosary with the visionaries to teach proper pronunciation. But, according to the children, when She herself took part, she only said the "Glory be to the Father."

making out that the Virgin of Garabandal seems to have been sent by the Vatican rather than from heaven; he speaks of the confessional as an offence against morals and juvenile candor. He describes the making of statues as a profanation of the laws of God, forbidden by the Bible; he gives an estimate of the number of medals manufactured, and the profits earned by this practice; he considers the references of the Virgin of Fatima to a possible conversion of Russia to be an invention on the part of Pope Pius XII in his anti-communist policy; he makes out the Blue Army of Our Lady of Fatima to be a mere political party, and one which invests millions of dollars in its publicity campaigns; he affirms that, out of gratitude for his declaring the dogma of the Immaculate Conception, Our Lady of Fatima ceremoniously addressed the Pope as "Holy Father"; he gives the Virgin's difference of apparel, as reported by the visionaries, as further evidence of fraud and fantasy, he says that a woman who has suffered greatly and died in her old age cannot appear young and beautiful; and so on.

I think all comment would be superfluous. The book is clearly nothing but a ferocious, savage, sacrilegious attack, packed with dire hatred and ill-will towards the Church, the Pope, the Virgin Mary, the angels, the Infant Jesus, the Holy Eucharist, Confession, the lot. The only thing that has come through unscathed so far is the Bible.

As for his language, he says in his prologue that it was not meant to be insulting. Yet, when speaking of the visible miracle of the Holy Communion administered by the angel to one of the visionaries at Garabandal, Monroy comments on the case in terms that the most daring pen would hesitate to reproduce.

Let this suffice. We could speak of celestial bodies and of why it is logical for the Blessed Virgin to appear younger than at her death; we could also explain why it is not absurd for Our Blessed. Mother to appear in different garb, just as nobody questions Monroy's own identity simply because he changes his overcoat from one day to the next. We could likewise show that the visionary at Fatima referred to the Holy Father using the common term that she customarily used for him, without this necessarily meaning that the Virgin herself employed it—although there would not be anything very extraordinary in her descending to the intellectual level of the visionaries so that they could understand her properly. Indeed, a thousand arguments could be used to refute Monroy's case. But, what would be the point?

The surprising thing about Monroy is that, after expressing himself in such terms as we have seen, he does not deny the existence of "supernatural" visions. What he denies is that such visions are the work of God. He considers the devil to be the prime originator of all apparitions, Lourdes, Our Lady of the Pillar at Zaragoza, Fatima, Garabandal and elsewhere. "The existence of the devil," he states, "cannot be denied if we simply reason a little. It would be the same as saying that evil does not exist, a statement that nobody would go so far as to venture. Nor can the devil be called a Christian invention. He is not; although the devil in Christianity is a being with his own personality, morally responsible for his own actions and totally different from the evil gods of ancient mythology, nevertheless, the belief in a negative force at work in the world is as old as the world itself."

"It is the devil who deceives the visionaries, who blinds the intellect in order to make it impossible to distinguish between the truth and falsehood. It is he who lays the foundations for apparitions. Once he has done the main share of the work, he stands back to let people's naivete, religious ignorance and the interests of Catholicism finish the job."

"All catholic authors with any sense of responsibility in their writing who have dealt with the subject of Lourdes concur in admitting the presence of the devil, although they hurriedly go on to give explanations which, far from clearing the matter up, simply serve to confuse the issue further."[†]

If this is so, how does he explain the devil's interruption during Bernadette's conversations with the Blessed Virgin? It is recounted in works on Lourdes as follows:

"During this apparition, all the witnesses could see how the visionary's face suddenly showed anxiety. Bernadette turned her head to the right, her gaze directed over the river Gave. She heard screams and sinister howls that seemed to proceed from the bowels of the earth. One of the voices shrieked: "Run away, run away!" The frightened young girl looked at the Virgin, who sadly turned her eyes towards the Gave and frowned. This sufficed to put the army of demons to flight."[††]

But, I should also like Monroy to clear up another point, for, to judge by his book, he has all the answers. Why does the devil disguise himself as the Blessed Virgin to convert sinners? Can the crowds that visit the shrines day and night, praying with their utmost faith, receiving Holy Communion, doing penance and seeking sanctity at all costs, be the fruit of a diabolical apostolate? If so, the powers of evil must have lost their wits; unless, of course, they are sick and tired of Hell and are trying to wangle their way into Heaven instead.

11.—I can quite understand indifference to apparitions. I quite understand many people not believing in them. I respect the attitude of those who are reluctant to admit what their reason cannot grasp. What I cannot understand is that, after an objective study of the apparitions of the Blessed Virgin, anyone should reach the conclusion that they are preternatural phenomena brought about by the spirit of Evil against God's will. The whole theory is hairbrained. It was Jesus Christ Himself who said in the Gospels: "By their fruit you will know them."

Let us forget about Monroy's book for the time being. We have studied and answered his main assertions and that is enough. We shall now look briefly at the apparitions approved by the Church and see how, in each case, there is something to show our reasoning minds as men of this world the "pointer" to belief. This will serve to comfort and bring added life to our faith. Afterwards, without definitely asserting or denying anything, we shall see what has been occurring in San Sebastian de Garabandal, the quaint hamlet in the province of Santander over which there hangs a giant question mark. Will Garabandal be a Spanish Fatima? For the time being, some of its episodes are being studied at length. Far be it from me to affirm or deny them. That is not my business. Judgment lies with Heaven.

[†]   Monroy, pages 109 and page 109
[††] "Estigmatizados y Apariciones", page 136

Aniceta Gonzalez, Conchita's mother

Conchita

A summer picnic: Conchita with her mother and her brother.

Jacinta's Father

Jacinta

Ceferino,
Mary Loli's Father

Mary Loli

Mari-Loli and Jacinta with Father Luna, leaving the Basilica of
Our Lady del Pilar in Saragossa (Oct. 1965).

Significant Lines of Conchita's Prayers

January 1, 1967

LORD, I pray for those who are spreading the message,
For those who do not accomplish the Message
For those who completely refuse the Message
Lord, I ask that your Message be spread,
Always, and more and more.

1967. . . . The four young girls will remain in the village for the summer until
the beginning of October. Conchita had expressed the wish to return to school
in August, but her mother prefers that she spends her vacation at home.
Conchita suffers from ulcers, Jacinta, from tuberculosis of the lungs and Mari-
Loli's condition is not too good.

In Rome January 13th 1966. Fr. Luna, Princess Cécile
of Bourbon, Conchita and her mother.

NUMERICAL INDEX

NUMERICAL INDEX Continued

◆ ◆ ◆

Made in the USA
Middletown, DE
17 September 2023

38648621R00125